The
Runes

THIS IS A CARLTON BOOK

This edition published by Barnes & Noble Inc.,
by arrangement with Carlton Books Ltd.

1995 Barnes & Noble Books

Text and design copyright © 1995 Carlton Books Limited

ISBN 1-56619-964-6

Project Editor: *Liz Wheeler*
Art Direction: *Zoë Maggs*
Design: *Susan Clarke*
Editor: *Kate Swainson*
Production: *Sarah Schuman*
Picture Research: *Charlotte Bush*

Printed in Italy

The Runes

Divine the future with this ancient Norse oracle

Horik Svensson

BARNES
& NOBLE
B O O K S
NEW YORK

Contents

And then the blue-eyed Norsemen told
A Saga of the days of old.
"There is", said he, "a wondrous book
Of Legends in the old Norse tongue,
Of the dead kings of Norroway, –
Legends that once were told or sung
In many a smoky fireside nook
Of Iceland, in the ancient day,
By wandering Saga-man or Scald;
Heimskringla is the volume called;
And he who looks may find therein
The story that I now begin."

And in each pause the story made
Upon his violin he played,
As an appropriate interlude,
Fragments of old Norwegian tunes
That bound in one the separate runes,
And held the mind in perfect mood,
Entwining and encircling all
The strange and antiquated rhymes
With melodies of olden times;
As over some half-ruined wall,
Disjointed and about to fall,
Fresh woodbines climb and interlace,
And keep the loosened stones in place.

Interlude to *The Musician's Tale: The Saga of King Olaf,*
part of *Tales of a Wayside Inn*, Longfellow

*Left: Detail of the Viking Sparlosa rune stone from Vastergotland,
with horse and other animals.*

introduction

Runes are an ancient form of writing that was used widely for thousands of years in the lands of northern Europe. A great deal of mystery surrounds their origins and use. According to Viking tradition, the word "rune" means a whispered secret. The Concise Oxford Dictionary informs us, in somewhat drier fashion, that the word "rune" means "any of the letters of the earliest Germanic alphabet used by Scandinavians and Anglo-Saxons from about the third century BC and formed by modifying Roman or Greek characters to suit carving".

In the West, most of us are familiar with the mythology of ancient Greece and Rome and knowingly incorporate their symbolism into our daily lives: "a young Adonis", the "martial arts", "jovial" characters and "venereal disease" are all references to Greek and Roman gods or goddesses. We make reference to the Norse pantheon even more often but without perhaps realizing so. In fact, the days of the week are named after Norse gods and goddesses: Tuesday stands

*The Rök stone , made by a father in honour of his dead son. In the
centre is an ode to Theodoric, king of the Goths.*

for Tiw's day, Wednesday is so called after the great god Odin,
Thursday is named after the powerful god Thor, and Friday takes its
name from the goddess Freya.

It is from the Norse culture that the runes come, and it was in
the old Teutonic world of northern Europe that the runes were venerated. They were the very soul of life for the ancient Teutonic
people, and encapsulated all of their mystical and mythological
beliefs. Now, after many centuries of being confined to some
dark recess, the runes are finally re-emerging as one of the
most powerful tools of magic that we have inherited
from our forebears.

norse mythology

The magical powers that the runes hold are embedded in Norse mythology, so to understand them it is important to have at least a slight understanding of the Norse legends. Legend has it that, generations after the demise of Asgard, home of the Norse gods, men went in search of the knowledge that had been lost from the golden age. After much toil they eventually found the goddess Saga, slumped on her throne in a dream-like state. She was woken by the questioning of the men and at last replied, "Are ye come at last to seek intelligence of the wisdom and deeds of your ancestors? I have written on these scrolls all that the people of that distant land thought and believed, and that which they held to be eternal truth. Ye will find much wisdom hidden therein, when ye can read the writing and understand the meaning of the pictures." The "pictures" to which the goddess Saga is referring are clearly runes.

Tales of the ancient Norse gods have their origins in the early home of the Aryan peoples – in India. These peoples lived very close to nature and believed that each natural phenomenon had its own personality. They would bow before the wind, worship the sun, fear the moon, and imbue every tree and rock with a life of its own. This approach to the world is now confined to the dictionary under the heading "animism", although the modern-day Gaia movement is making some headway in resurrecting it. The Aryan peoples gravitated northwards and, as they experienced increasingly harsh physical conditions, their animism increased in strength.

the creation myth

The ancient Norse culture built on this tradition, creating a mythology to explain the natural world. The Norse people believed that in the very beginning of time there was an enormous void or chasm called Ginnungagap. To the north of Ginnungagap lay Niflheim, the home of mist and darkness, while to the south lay Muspellheim, the home of fire and light. The mist from Niflheim drifted into the vast chasm of Ginnungagap and became blocks of ice. At the same time, sparks flying from Muspellheim fell onto the ice blocks and more steam rose and was formed into blocks of ice. In time, these blocks of ice completely filled the great void.

There also sprang two creatures, Ymir, the first of the ice giants and father of all evil beings, and the cow, Audumla, mother of goodness. From the perspiration of Ymir sprang two giants, and from his feet came the six-headed Thrudgelmir.

> In early times,
> When Ymir lived,   .
> Was not sand nor sea,
> Nor cooling wave;
> No earth was found,
> Nor heaven above;
> One chaos all,
> And nowhere grass.
> *Segmund's Edda*

At the same time, Audumla, licking the ice to survive, uncovered Buri, a divine creature and father to all that is good in the universe. Through the use of magic, Buri

11

produced a son, Borr. For a very long time war raged between good and evil, and neither side could gain ascendancy.

In time, Buri met and married Bestla, and they had a son, Odin, the greatest and strongest of all the giant peoples. When Odin came of age he led his brothers against the giants and slew the evil Ymir. The other giants were so stunned at Ymir's death that they stood stock still and were drowned in Ymir's gushing blood. Only two giants escaped: Bergelmir and his wife. They fled to the farthest corner of the universe and set up home, calling it Iotunheim.

Odin on his horse, Sleipnir is welcomed into Valhalla.

Odin rolled Ymir's body into the chasm and from it he created the universe. In the centre of the universe he created Midgard, the home of men, from Ymir's flesh. The hills and mountains were made from Ymir's bones, the stones and rocks from his teeth, and the grass, trees and shrubs from his hair. Midgard was surrounded by a sea of Ymir's blood, and the whole world was protected by a fence made from Ymir's eyebrows. Over this world, to create a sky, Odin placed Ymir's skull supported by four strong dwarves – north, south, east and west. As a final gesture, Odin scattered Ymir's brains inside the hollow of the skull to become white clouds.

But this world was still dark. To create light Odin took hold of some sparks from Muspellheim, the home of fire and light, and hurled them into the sky, creating the stars. At the same time, he decided to differentiate night from day. He took two large sparks from Muspellheim and set them in golden chariots to become the sun and moon. The chariot of the sun he gave to a beautiful young woman who had the power to see that the light of the sun shone clear and bright. In the other chariot he placed a handsome young man who had responsibility for the moon.

For a time both sun and moon were visible in the sky simultane-ously. However, then the giants exiled in Iotunheim saw these wondrous developments and determined that Midgard should be plunged back into darkness. So they sent two wolves, Skoll and Hati, to devour both the sun and moon. The two chariots fled from the wolves and, according to ancient Norse legend, will do so for ever more – moving continuously across the sky just in front of the ravening wolves.

Having achieved all this, Odin and the other gods decided to survey their work. The first thing they saw was that maggot-like creatures – black ones and also white

13

ones – had infested Ymir's body. Ever creative, Odin and the other gods transformed the white maggots into elves of light who would henceforth take care of everything that grew and who would live in Alfheim – between the earth and the sky. The black maggots were turned into elves of darkness, who were to live beneath the ground and be highly skilled in mining and in the crafting of all materials (similarly to the dwarves of Tolkien's Middle England).

Odin went walking through Midgard with the gods Honir and Loki. They came across two beautiful trees and decided to create new life from them: Ask and Embla, the first human beings from whom all others are descended. Odin's work was almost done. Finally he created the great ash tree, Yggdrasill. This giant of a tree had three roots – one in Midgard, one in Niflheim and one in Asgard – and was of such a size that its branches hung over Odin's halls in Asgard. It was from Yggdrasill that Odin first saw the runes and was able to reach down and grab them, giving the tree a special place in the mythology of the runes.

Etching of the great ash tree Yggdrasill.

the triumph of good

One of the great gods of the Norse pantheon was Balder, son of Odin and Freya, and a god of light. He was apparently beloved by all the gods except Loki, who was beginning to resemble Lucifer in his love of evil for its own sake. One night, Balder dreamed vividly of his forthcoming death and was so disturbed that he shared his dream with the other gods. His mother, Freya, was deeply upset and resolved to approach every living thing on heaven and earth to make them swear never to harm Balder.

The evil Loki, being punished for his wrong-doing, is comforted by his wife.

It appeared that Balder was invulnerable after this. His fellow gods would throw spears at him for fun, knowing that he could not be hurt. However, Loki transformed himself into an old woman and, using all his trickery, discovered from Frija that one living thing had failed to swear never to harm Balder: a sprig of mistletoe growing on an oak tree at the gate of Valhalla. Loki found this sprig and deceived the blind man, Hod, into throwing it at Balder. The mistletoe went straight into Balder's heart and killed him instantly.

This caused the gods a great deal of grief, but they refused to accept Balder's death as final and sent Odin's son, the messenger Hermod, to see Hel, ruler of the underworld, to plead for Balder's life. Hel replied to Hermod that if Balder were as beloved as he claimed, all living things would weep for him, and she would then release Balder. Hermod returned to the gods and told them of Hermod's decision. They in turn sent out messengers to every part of the land to request every living thing to weep, and they all agreed.

On their way home, however, the messengers discovered in a cave a giant woman called Thokk, who refused to weep. Balder was therefore confined to the underworld. Some time later at a feast of the gods, the evil Loki became drunk and arrogant and let it be known that it was he who had taken the shape of Thokk and thus condemned Balder to Hel's world. In their anger, the gods seized Loki and bound him in chains in a cavern where he would stay until the end of time, guarded by a venomous serpent. Loki broke free, however, and escaped to the land of the frost giants. From this point in Norse legend it became clear that the prophecies of the end of the world would come to pass.

There followed three terrible winters, with no summer to give respite from the interminable cold and dark. At the end of the third year, Skoll, the wolf who chased the

The great god Thor, creator of life, reconstructs the globe.

sun, caught up with the chariot and devoured the sun. In turn, the other wolf, Hati, devoured the moon. The stars finally went out and darkness once more ruled the universe. The final battle, "Ragnarok", began when all would be swept away in an orgy of blood-letting. Iormungard, the Midgard serpent, arose from the water and advanced on the land. Hel came out from the underworld with the hound Garm to join her father, Loki. All the frost and storm giants came out of Iotunheim to wage war on the gods.

From his guardian post on Bifrost, the rainbow bridge between Midgard, the world of men, and Asgard, the world of the gods, Heimdall saw what was happening and knew that the time had come to blow his horn. It lay at the base of the giant tree, Yggdrasill, for use only when the end of the world was nigh. There followed the most fearsome and hard-fought battle in which all were to perish. Odin fought with

Viking bronze statue of the fertility god Frey.

Fenris-wolf and was killed, to be avenged by his son, Vidar. Thor attacked the Midgard serpent with his hammer, Miollnir, and slew the dragon, only to be killed by its venomous breath as it expired. Tyr inflicted on the hound Garm a mortal blow but was mauled to death as the hound slowly died. Loki and Heimdall fought each other to the death, as did Surt and Frey, the god of fertility. When the battle was over and the ground strewn with dead, the fire from Muspellheim swept over everything and the waters flooded the land and obliterated all signs of life.

This is not the end of the tale, however. Out of the ashes of the old world arose the new. This is the ancient divine drama of creation, corruption, purification and renewal. "The Earth rises green and blooming out of its ruin, as soon as it has been thoroughly purged from sin, refined and restored by fire". The couple Lithrasir and Lif escaped the

holocaust by hiding in the great ash tree, Yggdrasill; Balder was released from Hel; and many other gods resumed their lives in Asgard. The corruption, hatred and misunderstanding had been swept away and a new golden age dawned.

Discovery of the Runes

I hung from a windswept tree.
I hung there for nine days and nights,
Gashed with a spear,
An offering to Odin,
A sacrifice to myself,
Bonded to the tree which no man knows,
Or whither its roots may run.

No-one gave me bread,
Nor gave me drink.
I peered down into the depths and
Snatched up the runes,
And with a fearful scream
Fell into a swoon.

After I began to thrive,
My wisdom thrived too.
I was joyful and I prospered.
One word led me to another,
One deed led me to another.

"The Speech of the High One",
The Poetic Edda, c. 1200 AD

This poem describes an event that can be seen in the Tarot card "The Hanged Man", or perhaps more obviously in the tale of Christ's death on the cross. Similar tales of initiation can be found in every corner of the globe and are still very much alive in the Fakir tradition in India. The man is suspended from the tree and through deprivation turns his mind to his own inner depths. He reaches a shattering enlightenment as the illusions of life are stripped away; the runes symbolize this self-discovery. He picks them up, a sign that they were not created as such but rather discovered.

Runic ring found in Norway.

history of
the runes

The Germanic "alphabet" was called "futhark" after the first six letters, like the Greek alphabet named after the first two letters – alpha and beta. There are a number of variants of the runic letters, but the

Runes and related magical sigils.

three main groups are the Germanic Futhark, the Anglo-Saxon Futhark and the Scandinavian Futhark. The Germanic Futhark consisted of 24 letters or symbols divided into three groups of eight, known as *aettir*. The numbers three and eight have special symbolism in the Nordic culture, and the three aettir were named after the Norse gods Freya, Hagal and Tir. An extra, twenty-fifth rune represents the unknowable and divine which permeate every part of life.

The Anglo-Saxon Futhark had 28 symbols, which later extended to 33. The Scandinavian Futhark was comprised of only 16 symbols, but these appear to have had double, and in some cases triple, meanings. The other futharks seem to be not real alphabets at all. There is debate over which was the original futhark, and as there is little or no evidence to help us, we are forced to speculate. The general consensus is that the Germanic futhark is the oldest and the one from which all the others derive.

A considerable number of runic carvings remain to this day. They are to be found in many parts of Europe, stretching from Scandinavia in the north, westwards to France, eastwards to Russia, and as far south as Rumania, but they are found in greatest concentration in Britain and Scandinavia. About 50 exist in Britain, some on stone and others on objects made out of other materials, such as whalebone. Denmark has about five times this number of carvings – about 250 – largely made in stone and dating from the tenth or eleventh centuries. Sweden, however, has almost ten times more carvings than Denmark – about 2,400.

Although south-western Denmark appears to be the "cradle of the runes", it would seem that this is not their place of origin. Much of the archaeological work carried out in recent years shows that the runes were known and widely used in south-eastern Europe, and it is generally under-

Scholars bear large sticks inscribed with ancient runic writing.

stood that the gothic writing that hails from that part of Europe was to a great extent constructed from the runes.

It is generally accepted that ancient Greece was the most likely source of the runes as they show striking similarities to the letters of the Greek alphabet. The underlying theory is that gothic merchants from south-east Europe learned both Greek and Latin in their travels, and on their return home created the runic stave alphabet – a sort of imperfect Greek with a blend of Latin. Separated from the influence of the classical world, runic writing began to be used primarily for inscriptions in wood, metal or stone.

Another theory places the origin of the runes in the ancient Etruscan language, as many correspondences between the two can be observed. The Etruscans inhabited the north of what we now call Italy, and the Goths inhabited adjacent lands. There is some evidence to suggest that the Goths adopted the Etruscan alphabet, at least in part. A third theory links the runes to the Hallristingnor carvings. These were

23

found in north Italy and the southern Germanic lands, and are believed to date from the early Bronze Age. Some of the carvings take the exact shape of runes.

The simple truth is that, at present, there is no way of knowing exactly where the runes originated. They are certainly ancient: the very earliest runes were written from left to right, as were other ancient languages. Part of the difficulty in locating their point of origin is that early runes were almost certainly engraved on wood, which decomposes easily and therefore leaves no evidence. This might explain the angular shape of the symbols, however, as the carver would have been very careful not to split the wood and would have simplified the job by working within the grain. It is also quite probable that, as part of the ceremony of using the runes, they were burned once the rite had been concluded.

the struggle for survival

As Christianity spread northwards, erection of rune stones eventually died out. The church made it its business to outlaw the use of runes and to destroy all evidence of their existence. This eradication of a culture was achieved by usurping it. Churches were built on sacred sites, and existing pagan festivals such as Ystre (Easter) and Saturnalia (Christmas) were simply borrowed for the Christians' own purposes. Ystre was an ancient pagan god of fertility, and the spring-time festival was a celebration of the rebirth of life after the cold death of winter. Christians lifted this festival and replaced it with their own rebirth festival to celebrate Christ's resurrection. In southern Germany the church went so far as to ban the use of the word Wodenstag (Wednesday) as

it means the god Woden's day, and to this day Germans still use the replacement word, Mittwoch, meaning the middle of the week.

The early Christians engaged upon a consicous programme to wipe out loyalty to any gods but their own. There would be no celebration, no magic ritual, no worship of any kind unless it were sanctioned by and for the Christian church. However, it took some time for the church to get a grip on the northern parts of Europe, so the use of the runes, the open worship of pagan gods, and magic ritual carried on there as normal until at least the beginning of the second Christian millennium. Yet, once the church was firmly established it went about its business of systematically eradicating pagan practices and outlawing use of the runes. It proved to be a lengthy operation, however, as runes were still being used in the seventeenth century, although by this time they had largely been driven underground.

The Christian church was in the main extremely effective in its destruction of the runic culture as it left a dearth of information about the depth and breadth of use of the runes. Out in the backwoods, however, away from the apathy and cynicism of the industrial cities, some of the ancient beliefs might well have survived almost intact up until very recent times.

While the church eradicated use of the runes themselves, it did not manage to control use of the actual runic symbols. In medieval times the people responded to the intransigence of the church by incorporating the runic symbols directly into their own half-timbered houses, placing the timbers in the plaster in recognizable rune configurations so that the inhabitants would have the power from those runes bestowed upon them. To this day there is a great number of houses all over northern Europe in which runic designs are still visible.

The problem with an oral tradition such as that of

the "whispered secret" runes is that it is ultimately dependent on social stability. Once society started to fragment and children left their homes to find their fortune in the big city the traditional knowledge soon began to disappear. The runes were not lost entirely, however, as they were rediscovered at the turn of the twentieth century in the great late-Victorian occult and spiritualist revival.

Unfortunately, the runes then went through a dark period as Hitler and the Nazi party used them as propaganda tools for their own political aims. The instantly recognizable Nazi symbol, the Swastika, was an ancient sun wheel symbol used all over the world, and in that particular form was well known in northern Europe. The Nazis reversed the direction of the wheel, with obvious implications. They demonstrated by this their assumed mastery over the sun, and turned a positive symbol into a feared one.

Perhaps the most obvious use of the runes in the Nazi hierarchy was the symbol worn by the Waffen SS. This was quite clearly a double Sigel (see page 61). Bearing in mind that the Sigel is again a positive, solar symbol with implications of power and victory, this was a conscious debasing of the ancient symbol. Largely owing to the Nazi subornment of the runes, they became once more confined to the dark. It is only in recent years that they have begun to re-emerge and be properly understood.

how the runes were used

Owing to the lack of material historical evidence, there has always been much discussion about how much the runes were part of everyday life. It is generally assumed that they were used only for magical purposes, especially

as talismans. It has also been difficult to discover why the Norse and Saxon peoples believed so fervently in the powers of these mystical symbols. However, there is some evidence to suggest that they were used in the same way as every other written language. The argument presumes that the "paper" of the day would have been either bark or parchment and that these would have rotted away, leaving us with no physical proof of their more everyday uses. It is clear, however, that the peoples of northern Europe used carved symbols in their daily lives and that the dividing line between these and the new symbols of the "alphabet" was, at first, not very clear.

The main reason for believing that the runes were used for mundane writings is the very existence of several different futharks. If the runes were purely magical, then there would have been no need to have a number of variants. In other symbolical languages, such as astrology, the symbols have remained essentially unchanged for many thousands of years. However, this argument is not as compelling as it might appear because another symbolical language, the Tarot, has retained great similarities over the last few hundred years at the same time as fostering variants.

The simple truth is that we do not have a complete historical picture. Many aspects of the Germanic pantheon and associated myths are, at present, lost to us. In the same way, we do not have full knowledge of how the runes were used. That they were in common usage across northern Europe from the Bronze Age up to the seventeenth century we do know, but the extent and scope of their usage is still shrouded in mystery.

the people
of the Runes

The Romans regarded all other races as barbarians but they did hold the Germans in very high regard for this people had, by the standards of those days, quite a complex and sophisticated society. The Germans lived in well-built houses, in organized villages, and on efficiently run farms. Each household possessed a number of out-houses which they used for storing food, baking bread, or as busy workshops. Despite being strong enemies, the German people and the Romans traded extensively with each other in silver, jewellery, pottery and even weapons.

Much of the information that is available to us today concerning the Germans comes from Cornelius Tacitus – a Roman soldier who later became a Roman Senator. He writes in 98 AD that the Germans fought their battles naked or wearing only a short cape, and that their weapons consisted of a short-bladed sword called a seax, a short spear that could be used as either a javelin or a stabbing tool, and a double-headed axe. The German army was led from the front by the nobles, and Tacitus tells us that they often took sacred emblems with them. They were doughty fighters and not easy to overcome, most particularly because they took their women to the battlefield to scream and shout encouragement, even baring their breasts – presumably to excite their menfolk to greater deeds in expectation of the pleasures to follow. The Germans were dismissive of death and liked to face it with utter defiance – particularly on the battlefield.

Tacitus also narrates that the Germans loved, above all, to feast and make merry. Hospitality was highly prized, and no-one would be turned away from their door

– indeed, every stranger was a friend. Tacitus makes detailed descriptions of how the Germans used runes, saying that from his observations they placed very great importance on the runes and used them for all manner of occasions.

At that time, the Romans had become corrupt and indulged in every form of sexual licence. By contrast, the Germans were a highly moral people for whom monogamy was the norm. Due to their shamanistic tradition (the religious tradition in place in many parts of pre-Christian Europe), the Germans saw sex as an almost mystical act in which life was both given and received. A concept that is central to the understanding of the German people and the runes themselves is that a gift demands a gift – that they could appease the gods by leaving gifts for them but that there would be a price to pay, if not now, then certainly in the afterlife for receiving a gift. In higher society, if a person received a gift from somebody, for whatever reason, he was obliged by custom to give something in return.

the tribes people

As the Roman Empire began to implode, in the fifth century the German tribes took the opportunity to grab large chunks of territory for themselves. The alliance of German tribes, named the Vandals, expanded southwards very rapidly, sweeping away all in their path. During this period the Saxons and the Angles in the north conquered Britain. They had gone there at the request of the British kings to act as mercenaries against the marauding Picts and Celts, but, when their job was done and they were asked to leave, they decided to stay and claim the country as their own. They then proceeded to drive north the

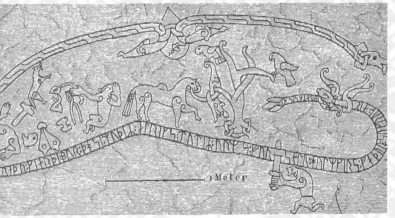

The Ramsundsberg, with scenes from the Saga of Sigurd Fanisbane.

Celts and the Picts until they reached the region of the present Scottish–English border. England was divided into seven areas. The largest ones were Northumbria to the north; Mercia being the great central swathe of the country; Wessex in the south and west. Considerably smaller were Essex, Sussex, Kent, and East Anglia, where the land was seriously water-logged.

We have a good deal of evidence to suggest that the use of runes was widespread among the German peoples of this time. One of the most important functions of the runes was to imbue weapons with special powers, and to this end runic inscriptions would be carved on swords and spears. Despite their conversion to Christianity, the Saxons continued to use the runes in much the same way as they had before.

The Saxons were, however, slowly overcome by

Rune stone from Skane, showing Fenrir, whose coming was said to foretell the waning of the gods' power.

the piratical Danish Vikings who pillaged and plundered the British coastline at will. Eventually the Danes expanded their on-shore territory until, by the end of the ninth century, a great part of Britain was under the Danelaw. Like the German tribes who conquered Britain earlier, the Viking peoples were well versed in the use of runes and had a well-organized society, so there was less a clash of culture than there was of swords. However, this was all to come to an abrupt end when William stepped ashore with his Normans in 1066, bringing with him the heavy hand of Catholicism and a return to the Latin language, in the form of early French.

The Normans and the Saxons may have originated from the same Germanic tribes but had grown in entirely different ways. For a very long time the invading Normans were widely detested by the Saxons, not least because

they seemed determined to wipe out all the ancient practices which they regarded, in their pristine Christian shells, to be nothing short of barbaric witchcraft. Naturally, evidence of the use of runes starts to disappear quite rapidly from this point onwards, although it has been found that some rural communities still used runes as late as the seventeenth century. Archaeological evidence of the runes can answer questions about how far the Germanic peoples travelled across Europe, and shows that they pillaged, traded and trekked for enormous distances and even reached North America.

The German tribes appear at first glance to be wild and vicious barbarians. In fact, this is far from the real picture. They had a strong belief in an afterlife and understood that their behaviour on Earth would determine where they went on to. If they lived a relatively decent life they would move on to Valhalla, where they could eat and drink all they wanted for all eternity. If they lived an unworthy life, however, they would be consigned to Hel, but this was not the same sort of place as the Christian Hell spouting its fire and brimstone. After all, the beloved Balder had been extricated from Hel so there was no reason to believe that this possibility was not open to all. However, in the great scheme of things, the behaviour that would be taken into account to determine whether Valhalla or Hel was your ultimate destination would only be that perpetrated within your own society. Any raping or pillaging carried out on another society did not count because the victims were by definition barbaric foreigners.

The runes affected not only the warrior culture and the morals of the Germanic peoples. Their culture was rich in poetry, artistic and literary works, some of which have survived to this day. The belief of the German peoples in the magical, spiritual power of the runes to bring goodness is the bedrock on which their artistry was built.

understanding
the runes

Above all, the runes are steeped in nature and symbolize the power exhibited by different elements of nature – the wind, the sun, ice and rain, for example. Therefore it is impossible to understand the runes by adopting an intellectual approach. The peoples of northern Europe led lives that were extremely close to nature and dominated by these elemental forces. As in many other ancient cultures, nature and the gods were considered to be one and the same thing. Each god symbolized a different element of the natural world and was believed to be responsible for the creation and continuation of his or her natural phenomenon. For example, to the Germanic peoples thunder was believed to be an action of the god Thor.

This can be quite a hard concept for the modern mind that is trained in logical, empirical thinking to grasp, but it is essential for understanding and using the runes effectively. In ancient times, the runes, by symbolizing these elemental forces, allowed the user, or querent, to make direct contact with the forces of nature, and thus perhaps to gain some insight into how the patterns of life were unfolding so that they could take the necessary steps to ensure survival. Life at that time was an extremely tenuous affair, and natural forces could cause death and disaster to those who were unprepared. To a certain extent, this still holds true today, witness the large-scale destruction caused by earthquakes, but we have such a sophisticated social system that, to a great extent, we are protected from the real chaos that nature can cause. Early peasant cultures were not: they were at nature's mercy.

One of the most important things to remember

about the runes is that the wisdom which the tradition contained was handed down from one generation to another orally – largely in the form of poetry to make it easier to remember. In ancient times, this sort of knowledge was not considered to be for everyone's eyes so it was never committed to writing.

the shaman

The shaman, who had been initiated into the knowledge of the runes, played a hugely important role in those times. He or she was the spiritual member of the community who gave each rune character its symbolic meaning and thereby its mystical power. The shaman was the most powerful figure in the tribal community as it was he, or she, who could determine and cure illness, foster fertility, ensure a good harvest, and solve many other concerns that were essential to everyday life, perhaps most notably protecting the tribe from its enemies – both the human and the animal kind.

For many cultures and many thousands of years, the shaman was the person who could bridge the gap between the world of the gods and that of ordinary humans and use their psychic ability to communicate with the spirit world. In that sense, they were conduits for nature itself, considering the gods and the elemental forces of nature as one and the same thing. In many parts of the world, shamans made a connection with the other world when they were in a trance-like state induced by drugs – especially those with hallucinogenic powers – or by dancing, fasting or conducting rituals.

Shamans were an integral part of the culture of the runes, yet they were specially selected, trained, and set apart from other people in the community. Both their

Stone relief showing a shaman who beats his drum (left) while a female (right) dances.

physical and mental powers had to be well above average in order to perform many of the rites and ceremonies involved. Although revered for their knowledge, shamans also inspired considerable awe through their apparently supernatural powers. In many parts of the world shamanism still exists, and shamans still live in self-imposed isolation living on a separate plane, wrapped in their magical universe.

Female fertility symbol, carved on the exterior of Kilpeck Church, Hereford and Worcester, England.

It was not uncommon for shamans to be in some way physically impaired at a time when it was almost impossible for anyone else to be crippled and survive. For ordinary people, disability was socially unacceptable. On a practical level, it was almost certain to lead to an early death and there was no form of social welfare in existence to make life more manageable. If you could not hunt or gather crops for the community you were an outcast. The only possible existence for a disabled person was to become a shaman – if he or she had the strength for such a demanding position. Even so, they would never be accepted into the day-to-day affairs of the community, regardless of their hugely influential role in community life.

The role of the shaman was kept in the family, passed down from generation to generation – from mother to daughter and from father to son.

natural forces

The runes are derived from natural forces, which the observant can see everywhere they look: in the shape of a stream as it flows through a field, at the point where the branch of a tree forks, or the random shape of stones on a beach. It is as if nature talks to us directly in the shapes of the runes. The knowledge they impart is also all around us, as long as we have the eyes to see and the mind to understand.

The runes have no history of being used in fantastic or magical enterprises: their powers are grounded firmly in the natural world. They could not – and cannot – impart amazing powers or huge success in the material world. They do not give political dominance or unearthly powers on the battlefield. Like nature itself, they are pragmatic and down to earth.

To this day, our language contains a number of little sayings that express the underlying philosophy of the runes – such as "nothing comes for free" and "what goes around comes around". If a king wished to win a battle and gain more territory, this desire would bring greatly increased responsibilities; if a peasant wished for more cattle he would know that this would create considerably more work for him. The people who used runes realized that there is always a price to pay for any gain in life. Because of this they took a less demanding approach to life than many people do in today's world.

meditating on the runes

The main source of information on the runes is the Anglo-Saxon rune poem which was translated by monks from Old English into Latin. It would appear that this translation was not completely unbiased and that many Christian-style references found their way into the translation. Despite this, the essential message is still clear.

Wealth is a comfort to everyone,
Yet each must give freely,
If he will glory in heaven.

The wild ox is fierce,
With horns above,
A bold fighter who steps the moor,
A mighty creature.

Thorn is very sharp to everyone,
Bad to take hold of,
Severe to those who rest among them.

Mouth is the origin of speech,
The support of wisdom,
And for everyone a blessing.

Riding in the hall is very pleasant,
It is more strenuous,
Sitting on a strong horse covering
The mile paths.

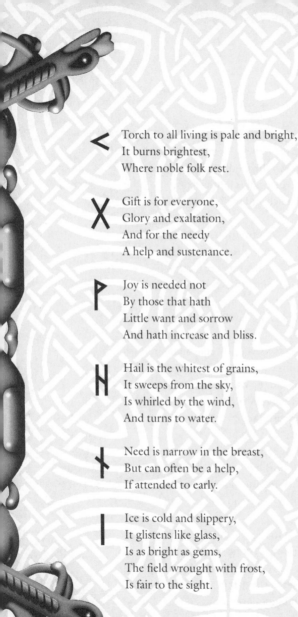

Torch to all living is pale and bright,
It burns brightest,
Where noble folk rest.

Gift is for everyone,
Glory and exaltation,
And for the needy
A help and sustenance.

Joy is needed not
By those that hath
Little want and sorrow
And hath increase and bliss.

Hail is the whitest of grains,
It sweeps from the sky,
Is whirled by the wind,
And turns to water.

Need is narrow in the breast,
But can often be a help,
If attended to early.

Ice is cold and slippery,
It glistens like glass,
Is as bright as gems,
The field wrought with frost,
Is fair to the sight.

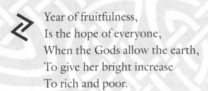

Year of fruitfulness,
Is the hope of everyone,
When the Gods allow the earth,
To give her bright increase
To rich and poor.

Yew is outwardly
A smooth tree,
Hard and fast in the earth,
The shepherd of fire,
Twisted beneath with roots,
A pleasure on the land.

Chess is ever play and laughter
To the proud,
Where the warriors sit
In the beer hall,
Cheerful together.

Sedge grows in the fen,
Flourishing in water,
Burning the blood
Of anyone who touches it.

Sun to the seafarer,
Is always confidence of nobles,
It is ever moving
And in the darkness
Of night never rests.

ᛏ Tir is a token
Which has a confidence
Of nobles,
It is ever moving
And in the darkness
of night never rests.

ᛒ Birch is fruitless
But bears twigs without increase,
It is beautiful in its branches,
Is laden with leaves,
Heavy in the air.

ᛗ Horse is the joy of nobles,
Where heroes wealthy on
Their horses exchange words,
To be restless is a comfort.

ᛗ Folk in their happiness
Are dear to their kindred,
Yet all must depart
From each other,
Because the gods commit
The body to the earth.

ᚠ Water to landfolk,
Seems tedious,
If they venture forth in an unsteady boat,
The sea waves will foam,
And the sea-horse heeds
Not the bridle.

ᛜ Ing was first seen among
The eastern Danes,
Departing over the waves,
His wagon ran behind,
Thus the warriors named him.

ᛞ Day is the gods' messenger,
The light of the gods,
Is happiness and consolation
To rich and poor.

ᛟ Home is beloved of everyone,
If they can enjoy their
Rights and labour
And prosper in peace.

Thomas Howard translation

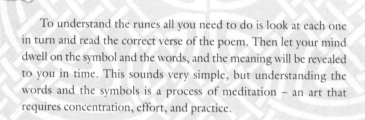

To understand the runes all you need to do is look at each one in turn and read the correct verse of the poem. Then let your mind dwell on the symbol and the words, and the meaning will be revealed to you in time. This sounds very simple, but understanding the words and the symbols is a process of meditation – an art that requires concentration, effort, and practice.

Viking rune stone from Gotland showing the god Wotan in procession.

interpreting the runes

In this section of the book we explain the meaning of each rune in detail. The main body of the text gives you an understanding of the essence of each rune followed by an explanation of the rune when it appears reversed. The interpretations given here are not meant to be definitive: consider them more as guidelines. As you work with the runes over a period of time you will develop your own understanding of them and what they symbolize individually in each reading. It is important to remember that no written definition of the runes can ever capture the inherent symbolism of the runes. The words written here should be treated as a springboard for your intuition and imagination. If you get bogged down by words they can act as a block to real understanding. Words are by their very nature reductionist and although they can be very helpful as a starting-point they must, as you gain in experience and knowledge, be left behind if your understanding of runic symbology is to grow.

 # feoh · cattle

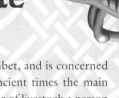

This is the first letter of the Germanic alphabet, and is concerned with worldly wealth and possessions. In ancient times the main measure of wealth and status was the number of livestock a person owned. Livestock was much more important than land as the ancient Germanic peoples were essentially nomadic.

This rune implies that wealth and success can be obtained through hard work rather than inherited wealth: cattle are not easy to look after and require considerable time and attention. This image is reinforced by the fact that, as the Germanic tribes gave up their nomadic existence and settled the land, cattle played an increasingly important role as workhorses in the cultivation of the land. There is also an image of conservation in this rune: the cow is a female symbol representing nourishment and continuity, and in ancient times would have been essential for survival in the long dark months of winter.

The ideas behind this rune are of gain being achieved against the odds, and also of advantage or vanquishing opposition. The counsel this rune offers, then, is that success may be achieved in the face of opposition, as long as a cautious approach is assumed.

reversed

If the upright Feoh implies expansion, vanquishing and gain, then reversed it signifies loss, restriction and being overcome by the odds. This always has a negative tone, but the negative effects are mediated by the surrounding runes. If the accompanying runes are positive, the reversed Feoh means only delays; but if they are negative, this indicates that matters are beyond repair and there is no hope of a satisfactory outcome. This applies not only in financial matters but also in affairs of the heart, perhaps signifying the end of a relationship.

UR · AUROCh

The auroch was a wild bison that used to roam the countryside of ancient Europe; now it is extinct. While Feoh represents the domesticated, Venusian nature of cattle, Ur represents the wild and martial side – the bull as opposed to the cow. In ancient Germany, an initiation rite required that each adolescent male took part in slaying an auroch. By the nature of initiation, this rune represents dramatic change, something that needs to be met without flinching. It could be a positive change, such as a new relationship or career. However, whatever it is, the change is nonetheless one that will require the shouldering of new responsibilities.

Ur implies that a challenge lies ahead – one of growing into new and larger shoes. However, if the querent approaches the situation with strength and determination – and has stamina – success is assured. He or she will need willpower to make lasting and effective changes, as they are something that the querent must bring about for themselves. This rune represents a testing time but one that can prove productive if "the bull is grabbed by the horns".

Reversed

A reversed Ur signifies that the querent is about to go through a major change that will not be for the better. It can also show that an opportunity is being presented that must be grabbed if disaster is to be avoided. The nature of the accompanying runes indicates whether the opportunity should be seized or, on the contrary, left well alone. Either way, the portents are not good. Reversed, this symbol indicates that the querent does not have the drive or will to deal with the current difficulties that he or she faces, and that the querent may be under the influence of some outside force – perhaps an illness or even another person.

 # th · thorn

At first glance the word Thorn appears to denote sharpness and pain, but it can equally be regarded as a protective shield or a warning. In this sense, the exact interpretation of this rune depends on the surrounding ones. The symbol of the rune resembles a hammer. In ancient Norse mythology, the protective god Thor carried a hammer, called Miollnir, and it was common for the ancient Germans to wear a small hammer around their neck to invoke his protective power.

This rune can denote great strength and good luck if the surrounding runes are helpful, and possible delay if they are unhelpful. On the one hand, it can mean that the moment holds great danger and that care must be taken. On the other hand, it may denote a warning, and often shows in readings when the querent has become overconfident of his or her own capabilities and is riding for a fall.

There is a strong element of luck associated with this rune, although it may appear in different guises. The saying "a thorn in my side" can be understood to indicate an irritation, but in the context of this rune the thorn is the obstacle that, once overcome, allows inner growth. This rune may also represent a test, because it may only be by "grasping the nettle" that progress can be achieved.

Reversed

Reversed, this rune indicates that the querent, faced with a difficult situation, is unlikely to be able to make good. It signifies an obdurateness that only makes the situation worse: all advice is studiously avoided and any helping hand ignored. Alternatively, the rune may show that luck has evaded the querent – perhaps more a comment on the querent's inner strength than on the situation. The querent's weakness and lack of dynamic will allows matters to drift out of control.

ansur · moutb

The Germanic tribes had a strong oral tradition: all their acquired wisdom and knowledge was passed down from generation to generation by the spoken word alone. As a result, the image of the mouth is very powerful. Even the Bible places great emphasis on the mouth: "In the beginning was the Word and the Word was God".

This rune can show that the querent is about to undergo an enlightening experience. It can be regarded as inspirational. It implies a state of reception rather than of actual speech and often appears in a runecast when the querent is about to undergo some form of test or interview; Ansur upright implies that the querent will do very well. This rune is also associated with apprenticeship, symbolizing that any learning process will prove highly productive. It can denote a chance meeting with someone who is able to shed new light on the situation.

The essence of this rune is advice and deliberation. It shows when hasty action by the querent will cause further difficulties. The best course of action is either to take the advice of elders or to spend time deliberating before taking action. Ansur is regarded as being closely allied to the planet Mercury, so when this rune shows in a reading there is a chance that it signifies a journey of some kind.

Reversed

If upright Ansur represents good advice then, reversed, it indicates bad advice. Whatever the situation, the querent should not listen too closely to what he or she is being told because the information is not in their best interest. The querent must be careful not to become so involved in the situation that they become unable to make clear decisions. Reversed, the implication is that the querent has become "unable to see the wood for the trees" and must therefore be objective and cautious.

Rad · Cartwheel

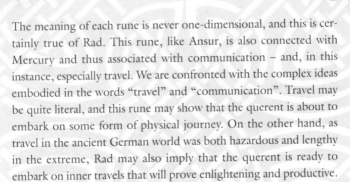

The meaning of each rune is never one-dimensional, and this is certainly true of Rad. This rune, like Ansur, is also connected with Mercury and thus associated with communication – and, in this instance, especially travel. We are confronted with the complex ideas embodied in the words "travel" and "communication". Travel may be quite literal, and this rune may show that the querent is about to embark on some form of physical journey. On the other hand, as travel in the ancient German world was both hazardous and lengthy in the extreme, Rad may also imply that the querent is ready to embark on inner travels that will prove enlightening and productive.

Unlike Ansur, which counsels caution, deliberation and taking sound advice before acting, Rad signifies a need to move now. The portents are good, it is time to leave behind the "I'm in two minds" scenario and make a decision. In addition, Mercury rules trade, so the appearance of Rad in a runecast brings economic implications. After all, the process of bartering is an essential process of trade, so Rad can show that some important business is on the horizon. As the central meaning behind Rad is travel and communication it also signifies the possibility of the querent receiving unexpected messages that will alter the present situation in a surprising way.

Reversed

In reverse, Rad shows that obstacles and delays associated with travel will be encountered. If the querent is about to embark on a journey, hindrances will probably stand in their way. When reversed, Rad also signifies that any travel will arise at a very awkward moment and leave the "home" situation exposed. It can further signify that the querent could expect a visit from a person who will be a considerable inconvenience.

ken · torch

The outer meaning of this rune concerns gifts. Ken is associated with Mars and the spring equinox, when the arrival of new life was traditionally celebrated by ancient peoples. By extension therefore, this symbol of fertility can also denote the imminent arrival of a child.

Ken is a masculine rune, and relates to the dominant person in the situation. If the querent is enquiring about business then Ken implies that the dominant person will be making offers. If this is the querent, the runecast shows whether the offer will be accepted; if the other protagonist is making the offer, the position of Ken in the runecast reveals whether the offer should be accepted. This is true in personal relationships, too, where Ken implies that the dominant partner is about to offer a gift. The surrounding runes reveal the motivation behind the gift, and whether it should be accepted.

Ken also has an inner meaning that concerns the acquisition of knowledge. In Scotland the word "ken" is still used to mean "know" or "knowledge". In addition, the ancient symbol of a torch denotes spiritual enlightenment – "the torch that lights the way". The querent may be required to use his or her own inner knowledge to light the way for others less fortunate than themselves.

Reversed

In reverse, this rune signifies loss. If the querent is involved in some potentially rewarding business deal the reversal of the rune shows that it will fall apart. If he or she is hoping for a child then it denotes false hopes, false alarms, and barrenness. It may even signify loss of employment or a relationship. It is not all doom and gloom, however, because this loss may be mitigated by positive accompanying runes, implying that any loss incurred now could well prove to be only temporary.

geofu · gift

When we want to indicate that two people are extremely close we cross our first and second fingers and say "they're like that". The symbol of a cross to signify union has been used since ancient times, and, with each stroke resting on the other, implies complete harmony. Geofu is associated with Venus, the goddess of love, so whenever this rune appears in a reading you can be sure that the querent is concerned with matters of the heart. In general, Geofu is a benevolent influence, although the surrounding runes explain more and may even indicate difficulties in relationships. The appearance of Geofu in a runecast often signifies that the querent is, or soon will be, in a generally peaceful and relaxed state of mind, at peace with themselves and the rest of the world.

On an inner level, this rune may be issuing a form of warning. Geofu shows that some gift – whether of money, love or wisdom – is likely to come the querent's way. As the saying goes, "nothing in life comes for free". All gifts imply that one has to give back – whether in this world or the next – at least as much as one has received. There is always a price to pay. In a sense, this rune reveals the immutable law of karma – "as you sow so shall ye reap". Therefore it is not wise to consider this rune as entirely positive. It may well prove to be very productive, but there are always attendant responsibilities that are to be ignored only at your peril.

wynn · joy

The Japanese concept of wa, "joyful harmony", comes close to explaining the meaning of this rune. The principle is of happiness derived from bending with the wind, implying that inner understanding and fluidity are important. On a more materialistic level, when this rune appears it implies that the querent will be successful in their present endeavours. The surrounding runes play an important role in interpreting the meaning. If Wynn is surrounded by "work" runes, for instance, this signifies that the querent will be successful in his or her chosen career and may well be promoted. If Wynn is closely allied with "travel" runes then it is certain that the querent will be highly successful in any venture that requires travel.

This rune is associated with the planet Saturn, and therefore implies that joy and fulfilment will be achieved through hard work. The symbol of the rune itself is likened to fruit on a tree, which in turn implies that matters that have been worked on for some time are about to come to fruition. Using the Saturnian analogy, this rune signifies both a conclusion and a new beginning: the mountain-top has been reached and so there is much happiness, but at the same time new vistas open up and new challenges wait to be conquered.

reversed

In reverse, the rune indicates that the challenges will not be met. The querent will either be daunted or will not have the right attitude to deal with them. The rune may also show that anyone else involved is not committed to the matter. So if the question concerns love, the querent's partner may be looking to move on. If it regard_ business, then there is every chance that a business partn_ looking to pull out of a deal. Great caution sh_ taken if further trouble is to be avoided.

hagall · hail

This rune always denotes limitation, and signifies that there is something or someone beyond the querent's control getting in the way of realizing his or her wishes. In ancient times, the natural world was dominated by the weather. Sacrifices were made to the gods in the hope of clement weather so that the crops could be safely gathered in. If crops were not harvested, the long dark winter quite simply brought ancient peoples to death's door. If the crops were severely damaged, stoic endurance was the only option for surviving the long, frugal winter. Of all the climatic conditions that could damage the crops, hail was, and still is, the worst.

Hagall shows that the road ahead will not always be simple and straightforward, and that many things are bound to occur over which we have no control. Hail storms are usually short, intense and unexpected, so Hagall implies that the querent will experience a sudden and unforeseen setback. It may often denote some physical check, such as unexpected illness or the unplanned conception of a child. In the face of such circumstances the querent may complain and feel put upon or take a pragmatic view that "these things are sent to try us" and attempt to reap a positive lesson from them.

Yet, not all delays and hindrances are necessarily unfortunate. The surrounding runes give a hint as to whether the unexpected situation will be pleasant or difficult to cope with. It may well be that forces beyond the querent's control prevent him or her from taking some particular course of action and that these obstacles later prove to have saved the querent from some disaster.

nied · necessity

On a material level, Nied denotes restriction. It is associated with the planet Saturn: the slowest-moving planet that the ancient Germans would have been able to observe. Saturn corresponds to our images of "old father time" and "the grim reaper". This planet represents the status quo, authority and structure. When Nied appears it shows that the querent is faced with a situation that he or she will not be able to change by drastic or headstrong action. Rather, the querent needs to have patience. Nied does not necessarily imply failure, but counsels that there are forces at work that are too strong and entrenched to be moved in a hurry. In affairs of the heart, Nied does not, as a rule, augur well as it is rather a cool and removed rune. It can, however, sometimes signify a distance between people – whether literally or metaphorically – that the querent seeks to overcome.

On an inner level, Nied signifies spiritual growth through hardship. Saturn is always a hard task-master and demands great sacrifice – as perhaps from a hermit or ascetic. However, deprivation can be a very good learning curve, if a little steep, at times. Inner strength is not built on resistance to, but acceptance of, the vicissitudes of life.

Reversed

In many sets of runes it is impossible to tell whether Nied is reversed or not, so in order to make a distinction you might be forced either to make some sort of mark on the rune itself or to rely heavily on your own intuition. If you perceive this rune as being reversed it denotes that the querent may have recently taken a rather flippant and thoughtless attitude and must now pay the dues. If the querent fails to change his or her approach forthwith the consequences could be dire indeed as the full force of the "establishment" comes down on them.

I ís · íce

At first glance one might assume that this rune is rather forbidding, as ice is obviously very cold and may be highly dangerous. That does not tell the whole story, however. Ice may in fact be protective: indeed, we use the expression "put on ice" to indicate that we want to store something away for later use. This rune counsels caution: the best course of action for the querent is no action. This is the moment to stop and metaphorically freeze all plans, as to continue would be fool-hardy – like stepping out onto ice.

The Is rune denotes that things have gone on for too long and with too much coldness for there to be much chance of any warmth returning. Sometimes this rune may denote the destruction of plans by stealthy and hidden hands: ice is easy to see once it has formed but only rarely does one see it develop, and it is strong enough to break almost anything in its path. Therefore the appearance of Is may also be taken as a serious warning. In questions that concern personal relationships, the appearance of this rune does not augur well for the future. Once ice has struck into the heart of loved ones there is little chance that matters will work out well.

The advice of this rune remains the same whichever way it falls, as its shape is the same in reverse. In essence, the advice is to put plans on hold and wait until the situation changes. Eventually there will be a thaw and then everything can revert to normal.

jara · harvest

Jara is a neutral rune in many ways, and this impartiality is represented in its design. It is almost a wheel and looks no different however it may fall in a runecast. The surrounding runes hint at the outcome. Its meaning is also closely linked to the wheel, inasmuch as it is concerned with cycles. Although the word harvest tends to have fairly positive connotations, there are in truth all kinds of harvest: certainly the bumper crops displayed in a church at harvest festival time but also the life sentence meted out to a murderer.

So the appearance of Jara in a reading implies a time of reckoning, when things have perhaps gone full cycle and must now be reviewed. In many instances Jara signifies legal matters, the general way of reckoning in our culture. Since this rune indicates "just desserts", justice is likely to be involved in some way. As Jara also governs every kind of contract, there could be a chance of some form of business deal or even a marriage.

On another level, this rune can represent disturbing forces at work, represented as it is by two interlocking forces whirling around each other. It is an indication of inner turmoil, of the querent being almost torn apart by opposing emotions, and yet still managing to keep them contained. This turmoil approaches resolution, but while this might produce a certain peace, some loss is also involved. Once again, the runes show us that nothing comes for free.

yr · yew

Yew was perhaps the most important wood to ancient northern peoples. It was the mother of the longbow, the weapon that brought them food and, in times of war, protection. Not only was the yew tree of immense practical value to these people but it also held mystical significance as a symbol of death and resurrection. It is still found to this day in many church cemeteries.

When Yr appears in a runecast it is generally a very positive sign. It signifies that the querent is within striking distance of his or her target and, with a steady aim, will achieve it before too long. Sometimes Yr may denote delay, but nonetheless the outcome is still more than likely to be positive. On a mystical level, Yr represents the ability to put one's inner self into stronger and safer territory. The yew tree is evergreen and highly flexible, yet very strong, and is excellent for making staffs which may, in turn, be seen as symbols of inner strength. The yew tree in a churchyard exists symbolically to direct the souls onward to the other side, revealing that Yr has more than one side to its nature.

As with Jara and Is, Yr shows no distinction whichever way it falls in a runecast. Because of this, particular attention must be paid to the surrounding runes in the cast, as they reveal the kind of anticipatory actions the querent should take to avoid problems. Yr shows that there is a way out of any difficulty as long as the situation is approached in the correct manner.

peorth · ?

The meaning of this rune has been left a question mark because in modern times we have no way of knowing its exact nature. It has been described variously as an apple, a chess piece, a dice cup, a tune, a hearth, and even a penis. This lack of clear meaning is apposite as Peorth signifies something unresolved in the querent's life, something hidden away that is about to surface. It may represent a secret, something the querent feels sensitive about. This can be a hint to the person doing the reading. When Peorth appears, it can signify that the querent is not being completely honest about the question and is really asking something else.

As a rule this rune has fairly positive connotations, implying that the secret about to be revealed will be helpful or pleasant to the querent. For instance, it can signify that affairs of the heart that the querent has been unsure of will be resolved to their advantage – and surprise. It can also denote an unexpected inheritance. In addition, this rune has associations with gambling, although the route by which this meaning is reached is somewhat dubious. However, on this basis, Peorth can mean that it is a good time for the querent to undertake some financial venture that might appear a little risky.

Reversed

In reverse, Peorth indicates that what is about to be revealed will be none too pleasant for the querent. If he or she has any dark secrets, a reversed Peorth signifies that they will be exposed. Alternatively, when reversed, this rune may indicate that someone with whom the querent is involved, either personally or in business, is not to be trusted and that the evidence for this will soon appear. In either case, the querent must arm him or herself for disclosures of a discomforting nature.

eolh · protection

This rune is like a protective charm, and whenever it turns up in a reading the message is optimistic. The origins of its name unclear and disputed. Some say that Eolh means "an elk", others argue that it refers to a particular kind of grass called elk-sedge, and yet others regard it as a reference to amber. Nor is the symbol itself free from dispute, with one camp regarding it as an outstretched hand, another seeing it as an antler, and yet another arguing that it is some kind of staff. However, it is agreed by all that this is a most auspicious and beneficial rune, no matter what place it holds in the cast.

Eolh signifies that the querent is shielded from danger or difficulty during the time span to which the question applies. It may also signify that a new influence – a beneficial one – is about to enter the querent's life. This could take the form of a new career, or perhaps just a new interest, and may even reveal a forthcoming marriage. It is also likely that this new influence, whatever it might be, will not arrive as the result of conscious reasoning and determination. This is a rune of friendship and protection but it is through one's inner self that this friendly influence is manifested. It is what the querent needs but also what the querent deserves.

Reversed

When this rune is reversed in a reading it signifies that the querent is being, or about to be, duped. People around the querent, whether in business or personal relationships, have their own agenda that is not of benefit to the querent. Eolh reversed indicates that the querent needs to take great care and caution because others do not have their best interests at heart; indeed, others may do their level best to ensure that the querent unjustly takes the blame for a mistake.

sígel · sun

This rune, by virtue of representing the sun, is closely associated with the astrological sign Leo, which is ruled by the sun. This gives considerable insight into its meaning. Leo is a sign that likes to enjoy life and have fun; it is also a very proud sign and one that likes to be at the centre of things, basking in peoples' attention.

Thus when Sigel appears in a reading it can imply that the querent has been overstretched of late and is in need of a rest, to take time away from the pressures of everyday life and just enjoy him- or herself. It may also signify that the querent is in a situation that he or she needs to take control of. Perhaps the querent has been worrying about something recently, yet was feeling unable to make any positive move to alter the situation, and this has left them feeling curiously out of sorts. Once again the advice must be to return to the centre of affairs and take control.

The sun has traditionally been associated with vitality and vigour, so the surrounding runes in a cast give some hint to the querent's state of health. On the other hand, if Sigel is close to very positive runes this means that the querent is at the peak of his or her powers. Sigel can further be seen as the principle of "the guiding light", the beacon that lights the way. So on the material level its appearance may well signify that the querent is in need of help, needing someone or something to arise and show them the way forward. This may also be true on a spiritual level, in which Sigel may signify that the querent should seek, or will soon find, a spiritual guide.

tír · creator

The god Tir is the original creator god who became replaced by Odin in Norse mythology. But Tir (or Tiw in the Anglo-Saxon – hence Tiw's day) was not the benign creator of the Christian church but a warrior god much more akin to Mars. Thus the appearance of Tir in any reading points to battles, competition and vigorous energy. In ancient times this rune would almost certainly have signified actual physical battle and the whole panoply of preparation associated with it – sharpening swords and axes, making bows and arrows, laying in stocks of food, and seeing to the animals, for example. This is unlikely today, but the analogy can be stretched.

Tir shows that the querent is about to embark on an enterprise that will require a great deal of energy – moral, physical or both. The enterprise will be competitive in some way, whether in business, the law courts, or in the form of moral argument that the querent needs to win. If the querent is involved in business dealings then Tir implies that there are likely to be boardroom battles and that it will be necessary to be well prepared. "Winning" is the clue to understanding this rune: blood may have to be spilled but victory must be assured.

reverseo

When Tir shows up reversed it signifies that the querent is in a rather weak frame of mind, lacking any real will power or motivation. It implies a certain expectant indolence, as if the world owed them a living and everything would simply turn up through no effort of their own. If the question concerns business then things will not get better until the querent gets a grip on themselves. In affairs of love it indicates difficulties ahead and a possible breakdown of communications, while in health it shows that the querent may be in a poor physical state.

beorc · birch

This rune is a fertility symbol, drawn to resemble a woman's breasts. In ancient times the birch was regarded as the tree of fertility, and being lightly whipped with birch twigs was supposed to increase vigour and fertility. This belief is still held in Scandinavia where, after a sauna, people are encouraged to roll in the snow and then endure a quick lashing with a bundle of birch twigs. The phallic maypole that was traditionally danced around as a symbol of new life, the coming of spring, and fertility in general was more often than not made of birch. So when Beorc appears in a reading it points clearly to inception, whether of a child, a project or simply an idea.

Beroc is generally auspicious. However, because it symbolizes the mother and, by implication, the child, there is an element of "nourishment" associated with it. Thus, even if the rune is essentially beneficial the new project will need the same kind of succour as an infant. Success will not come of its own accord: effort and attention will be required. This may explain the traditional duality ascribed to the birch, the "fruitless tree", implying that all is not quite as it seems and that success will be achieved only through genuine application.

Reversed

Reversed, Beorc becomes a symbol of sterility, implying difficulties and misunderstandings on the domestic front. Perhaps a desired pregnancy will prove impossible, or a current pregnancy be terminated. Alternatively, it can point to worries over children, especially in terms of health. However, the surrounding runes always give a much clearer picture. A reversed Beorc is not particularly malign of itself and requires other more ruthless runes to imply real trouble, while helpful runes definitely alleviate the situation.

eoh · horse

The meaning of Eoh is largely neutral, indicating travel and possible change. On the material level, it denotes change that is generally successful. Such change is unlikely to come as a great surprise as it is probable that he or she has already taken steps and is enquiring about its outcome. In these cases the signs are good. Eoh is associated with the planet Mercury so it has much to do with travel, and the word Eoh itself has been translated as "horse". Eoh may denote such simple travel as a visit to a relative, but it may also signify a change of home or neighbourhood.

On a more mystical level, Eoh signifies a need to establish strong connections between oneself and one's emotions. Horses are temperamental animals and need the right mix of encouragement and control if they are to be of value on a journey. The horse was sacred to the ancients, and both the sun and moon were pulled in their chariots across the sky by horses. As Michael Howard points out, one need look no further than the white horse of Uffington, England, carved into the chalky hillside to see how the ancient people of the North venerated this animal. The horse is a traditional symbol of power that can lead to liberation if understood and handled correctly.

reversed

When it appears reversed, the meaning of Eoh remains substantially the same as it does when upright. It signals travel and change, as before. However, in this instance the change may well not be for the better, may possibly not be made out of choice but necessity, and may perhaps even be totally unexpected. Alternatively, if the querent is planning to go on a long trip or begin some new venture it would be wise to put such plans to one side for now as they are unlikely to prove fortuitous.

mann · man

This rune teaches us that we are alone yet not alone. We are a separate entity but part of the human race and the universe. From a material viewpoint, when Mann appears in a runecast it tends to show that the querent has lost his or her way and needs to seek advice to bring some clarity back into the situation. Wisdom is required. This may not have to be found from others as it is possible that the rune is telling the querent to stop chasing his or her tail and look at the current situation with a cool and dispassionate eye.

Since this rune means mankind in general and has associations with the planet Saturn, its appearance in a reading may point to civic and social duty. It is easy to become self-absorbed and to forget one's wider responsibilities to family, friends and the less fortunate in society. Mann is a reminder that we do not live in a vacuum. Once again, this reflects the dispassionate nature of this rune: caring for others is achieved more easily if a certain distance is retained.

On a spiritual level, Mann goes in the other direction and shows us that sometimes it is necessary to put others behind us and tread a new and lonelier path if we are to progress.

reversed

In reverse, Mann shows that the querent is surrounded by people who either do not necessarily have his or her best interests at heart or are simply not about to lend a helping hand or offer sound, useful advice. There is someone, or a group of people, standing in the querent's way, and the querent will have to decide how best to tackle the problem. The accompanying runes show the way forward. A reversed Mann may also indicate that the enemy is within and perhaps that the querent should take a more positive and cooperative approach.

lagu · water

Lagu represents the hidden side of our nature. For thousands of years, water has been regarded as one of the four elemental forces alongside fire, earth and air. It is associated with the moon, which governs its movements and which in turn is associated with the feminine or passive and receptive principle. Thus, when Lagu appears in a runecast, it implies that the querent is either in a receptive frame of mind or that he or she needs to turn off the chattering of the conscious mind and listen to his or her inner voice – "intuition".

Some people might be defensive about the idea of being intuitive, and feel that the logical application of a rational approach is the way forward. Lagu says that this attitude only causes further difficulty. The querent would be advised to be flexible about problems at hand: if they flow with the tide rather than fight against it success is likely. Lagu signifies receptivity in all its forms so it can denote a perfect opportunity to "learn". This could mean anything from an academic undertaking to seeking spiritual advice. Lagu may also denote that any obstructions that have been standing in the querent's path will be washed away.

reverseD

When reversed, this rune invariably points to weakness and possible betrayal. In reversal the subconscious, or intuitive and receptive part of the mind, is turned upside-down, indicating that the querent has become mixed up and is about to get into real difficulty if firm and immediate action is not taken. It may be that the querent gives too much credibility to someone else or, more likely, that they give themselves an undeserved credibility. They may believe that they have great powers of intuition when they clearly do not. Or their intuition may be subverted so they attempt things that they will not be able to carry off.

ing · fertility

This is a primal rune whose symbolism is clearly that of female genitalia. The essential meaning of Ing is completion or, by implication, orgasm. Orgasm is, of course, somewhat double-edged, as is recognized by the French in their description of it as "le petit mort" ("the little death"). It is the desired goal that spends one's force. The appearance of Ing in a runecast is almost always a good omen. Only in very rare cases does it produce a bad result. It is also one of the runes that is unaffected by the way in which it falls, showing no difference whether it is upright or reversed.

On the material level, in some instances Ing may show that the querent has been undergoing some kind of difficulty and that the situation is now drawing to a close, with relief at hand. Since Ing was a fertility god and this rune is, at least symbolically, sexual, it can show the imminent birth of a child or perhaps of some new idea or venture. This is the inherent contradiction in orgasm – the "little death" that simultaneously plants the seed of new life. Pursuing the analogy of child birth, in most cases the birth of a child is a cause for great celebration and much happiness, so by implication the changes on the horizon for the querent will herald happiness and fulfilment.

On a more spiritual level, this rune shows that the querent is soon to reach a state of inner peace and quiet, of inner balance. In all cases time will tell whether this happy state is lasting or simply transitory, and the accompanying runes will give strong suggestions as to the eventual outcome.

ᛞ daeg · day

Like the sun rising, this is a rune of new beginnings, the dawn of new ideas. Daeg is a very optimistic rune and shows that good times are definitely on their way. Whenever it appears in a runecast it shows that the querent is moving into a period of growth in any area of life – perhaps business, family, or inwardly. The querent has probably been preparing for good times for a considerable while, and should not be surprised by the positive upturn in their life.

It is important to understand the symbology of the rune in terms of the Teutonic tribes. Living close to nature, and particularly living so far north, the beginnings of spring – with the sun climbing higher in the sky, the days lengthening, and warmth finally arriving after the long, cold, dark months of winter – would have been a magical annual reaffirmation of life. After the harsh winter barely surviving in their caves, at last they could move into the open, get some fresh air and sunlight, and look forward to being able to eat fresh food, especially fruits and vegetables. They would have had very little fresh food all winter and their health would be beginning to suffer.

Daeg is often more about a state of mind than material matters, and its appearance in a runecast often points to the querent deciding to bring change in his or her life, even if this is only a decision to be more accepting of what exists now. This process of inner acceptance invariably has a positive "outer" result. The philosophy of acceptance runs counter to modern attitudes which tend toward the combative. Yet, when faced with serious obstacles, success can often be achieved by "letting go" rather than putting up a fight.

othel · home

As the twenty-fourth rune, Othel encompasses several different but allied concepts. It certainly represents possessions and tends to represent land, buildings or more specifically the home – usually the most important possession we are likely to own and the greatest part of our estate that we leave to the next generation. If Othel represents money, then the likelihood is that it signifies money that is in some way tied up, such as wills, legacies or covenants.

Othel is closely associated with the planet Saturn, implying that the possessions it refers to carry some sort of restriction or limitation – hence its connection with land, which incurs duties and obligations, and cannot be packed up and moved about. This rune is also a symbol of ancestry, not just what we inherit in the form of the ancestral home and the bank account, but also the particular psychological traits that have been passed down from one generation to another. Othel makes us look at who we are, where we come from, and finally, where we are going. As with all Saturnian affairs, Othel carries the message of "karma" and reminds us that we should "keep our house in order".

Reversed

When Othel appears reversed in a runecast it implies that the querent will have to face alone whatever troubles lie ahead. There is no recourse to outside help. It indicates a certain finality, that the querent has no option but to square up to the situation and deal honourably with whatever life decides to throw at them. This may well mean failure, or simply delay, but there is no way of fighting the inevitability of events. The querent would be advised to take a very realistic approach and understand that there is no avoiding "karma".

69

wyrd · fate

This rune has no markings at all. In some ways it may be considered the joker in the pack because one never quite knows its meaning without looking at the surrounding runes in the cast. The essential message of Wyrd is one of immutable fate or karma. The querent is faced with an inescapable situation and will have to take whatever comes – there is simply no way out. This does not necessarily mean that what is about to be served up will be unpleasant. The rewards for behaviour, whether here or in the next world, are by no means all bad. Wyrd's blank face may also signify things that we must keep secret in our lives so that we present the same blank face to the world.

The appearance of Wyrd in a runecast does not presage doom but may in fact herald pleasant outcomes, depending on the context in which it appears. The surrounding runes point to the specific way in which things manifest themselves, and Wyrd states that it will happen; there is no argument and no escape. For example, if Wyrd appears next to a positive, financial rune then the querent can look forward to receiving money in the near future. If allied with a love rune then romance is certain to bloom shortly. If it is next to one of the more negative runes this can be a tough message for the querent to accept, but the inevitability of the situation has to be accepted.

using
the runes

Before using the runes it is important to get in touch with the energies they represent. Our forebears held an holistic view of the world, so succinctly put in the old adage, "as above, so below" before the scientific, empirical view of the world achieved the dominance it holds today. It is a sad commentary on modern life that such an holistic view of the universe is generally derided today. Neither have the established churches helped in this process: they have too much to lose if everyone can talk to their god without the intervening presence of a church official. There is little room left for the individual to commune with the natural god in the ancient ways.

The average querent today is interested in matters concerning their everyday life: variants on the themes of money/career, love/sex, and health. While these issues make up our day-to-day lives, such preoccupation with personal physical matters ignores the important question of the state of our spiritual life. Yet, because an accomplished practitioner of the runes continuously takes an holistic approach, he or she should be more than able to reach through to the "other side" and give the querent sound advice on more than one level at the same time. Anyone considering using the runes needs to develop a true feeling for, and understanding of, the way in which the energies of the universe flow through everything. Without this, the runes can become little more than a neat party trick.

This section of the book explores the philosophy behind using the runes; explains the significance of the equipment you need to cast runes; and shows how to cast and interpret runes in readings.

the concept of time

The question of how runic divination works – and indeed, whether it has any validity at all – has received much attention. Our common perception of what we call "time" is a useful starting-point.

In his book, *Time: The Ultimate Energy*, Murray Hope says: "At this point in the evolutionary history of our planet our concept of the nature of time has mostly been dictated by the subjective experiences of our life cycles. We tend to view time in linear terms as applicable to our own planet and solar system." In other words, we seem to be locked into a view of time that is largely dictated by our own life span. And this generally follows a pattern so apparently pre-ordained that we are even encouraged to plan for the end of our lives with life assurance and pension plans. William Shakespeare ably divided a person's life span into phases – the seven ages of Man in *As You Like It*: "At first the infant, mewling and puking in his nurse's arms, and then the schoolboy creeping like snail unwillingly to school" and so on.

Time that can be measured by the turning of the planet and translated into continuous viewing on the clock face is called "inner time" by Hope. He goes on to say: "The non-linear time that exists beyond the confines of our own little corner of the universe I refer to as 'outer time'. Outer time, not being subject to physical conditions as such, also embraces timelessness, and those subtle dimensions that are not concerned with the worlds of matter, about which our knowledge is purely speculative and therefore more metaphysical than physical."

It seems quite clear that we humans do have the capacity to move into this timeless world, but we require some sort of internal rewiring to move us beyond the

normal, everyday perception of time. To quote from *Time: The Ultimate Energy* once more: "Once the time-code has been cracked, vast energy fields, the nature and breadth of which we may not even have dreamed of, will be available for our use and we can only guess at which direction our handling of these powers may take once we have familiarized ourselves with their existence and obvious usefulness. But of course, having conquered the enemy and finally freed ourselves from the chains of inner time that have constituted our bondage during the particular evolutionary cycle through which we have been passing, we will, we hope, be wiser, more sensitive, and more spiritually mature."

In the second century BC, Plautus succinctly described how our linear perception of time is so restricting:

> The gods confound the man who first found out
> How to distinguish hours! Confound him too,
> Who in this place set up a sun-dial,
> To cut and hack my days so wretchedly
> Into small portions.

While the "time" we know and love so well has many undoubted uses, it also prevents us from seeing very clearly the universe in which we live. By breaking our perception of time we can use divinatory tools such as the runes to enter a new world. Meditation (see page 94) can also unlock the mind, giving access to a universe or power and energy not normally available to us.

the process of divination

So how does the process of divination really work? The old occult axiom "as above, so below" is the basis of all divination. It is easy to understand once we have got past the idea that time is linear. Instead, it can be seen as circular. If you were to stand at the centre of the circle you would have no sense of the past or the future because time would be all around you, as if it were all " the present". Alternatively, time can be thought of as a ball. If you cut a cross-section of the ball, every part of the past, present and future would be clearly visible. This view of time gets to the heart of the matter because it may be possible to measure time in terms of quality rather than the movement of hands across a clock face. In other words, the cross-section of time we cut out of the ball has its own special qualities that depend not on the hour of the day but on the universal energy flowing through it.

The runes simply reflect that energy. It is the role of the runecaster to be the agent through which this energy becomes visible. This also applies to using Tarot cards or interpreting tea leaves. However, because the runes have such a long tradition, are made from natural materials, and are engraved with special symbols, it is easier to get in touch with the quality of time and the energies using the runes. The runic symbols talk to the unconscious mind in a way that words cannot. Each one contains a series of meanings, and a runecast will create a logical connection between each one even where the conscious mind sees none. For instance, the rune Jara has many different layers of meaning: a stroke of good luck, financial reward, just desserts, a contract or business deal, and a marriage. On the spiritual plane,

it may also mean that the querent is about to embark on a new phase of their spiritual path. Each rune is modified by those coming before and after so it is essential to be in tune to see which elements of each rune are being expressed.

To the modern scientist who views the universe in terms of atoms, sub-atomic particles and quarks, for example, such a view is nonsense. However, the psychoanalyst does not have such a problem with it. Carl Jung, the father of psychoanalysis, did a great deal of work on the myths of mankind and came to realize that there were not as many variations as might at first appear. He found that all human myths and fairy tales – from whatever part of the world they came – reflect and enhance each other. Jung created a brand new mythology for the 20th century, containing its own mythological pantheon which he called "archetypes". Whether we call these gods, myths or runes does not matter in the least; what is important is to see them as the way in which the prime force of the universe is manifested. A parallel with the Christian myth may even be drawn, wherein Jesus could be seen as the prime force and the 12 apostles as his manifestation.

The power of the runes rests in their very "earthiness". In times past, people did not perceive Earth simply as the land on which we live, but rather as a living, breathing creature itself, no different from all the other living creatures that travelled with her through the universe. This concept has had a rebirth recently in what is known as the "Gaia" theory. In essence, this is a return to the holistic views held from time immemorial and disrupted only by the advent of science. The runes, being made from the earth itself, in the form of stone, clay or wood, have a natural resonance with the earth and, by extension, with the whole universe. This explains the rather pragmatic approach with the ancient Norse peoples had to the runes. They believed very

strongly that "a gift deserves a gift" or, to be contemporary, "there is no such thing as a free lunch". The runes draw upon the universal energies and embody them; but in using the runes those energies must be returned to the earth, or the process will become corrupted.

But, asks the determined cynic, if the process of divination works, and most especially using runes, doesn't that mean that life is pre-destined? And if it is, what is the point in doing anything at all? This has been debated since humans first discovered that the world is not, in fact, flat and that the sun does not revolve around the Earth. There is, and never has been, any problem about resolving the apparent problems between free will and determinism. The interaction between the universe and an individual creates a set of circumstances that can be loosely called "karma". These circumstances can be blindly followed or altered by the use of free will. The art of prediction aims not to lay down a specific outcome so much as to point out the dynamics of the existing situation and indicate a number of possible, or likely, outcomes. By understanding what is happening here and now we can make conscious decisions to affect the outcome of events rather than to be driven blindly by them.

Divination propounds that there is only a limited number of circumstances and possibilities available at any one moment in time for a given individual or group of people. Either singularly or plurally, their free will is limited – but not determined – by that set of circumstances. To couch it in other terms, it is like saying that you can talk to only one god at a time but in a variety of different ways about a range of subjects; or, in psychoanalytic terms, that you can act out only one archetype at a time but in a multitude of ways. Once you understand which god you are talking to, or which archetype you are acting out, free will allows you to select the best possible outcome from those available.

the runestones

This book comes complete with a set of terracotta runes in a hessian bag. If you do not already have your own set of runes, use these to get you started. You should feel comfortable with your runes. Become accustomed to the feel and shape of them; allow them to be special to you. It is extremely important that you do not let other people handle your runes or their energy will become dissipated.

When you are practised at handling and using the runes that are provided in this pack you may like to make your own runes. If you do this, you can choose your own material and imbue them with your personal vibration. There is no doubt that natural materials such as wood, stone, clay, terracotta or, for the less squeamish, bone are preferable to man-made materials, such as plastic, because the runes are so closely allied to natural forces.

choosing a material

The most commonly used materials are wood, pebbles or ceramics (like those in this pack). Wood has the obvious advantage of being easy to cut into shape as well as being very easy to carve. Choose wood from either a particular species of tree that has some significance for you, or even from a tree that you have known and loved for some time. Some people prefer to take wood from a living tree on the basis that the wood is then "alive", while others prefer to search for pieces of dead wood that lie on the forest floor. When taking wood from a tree, do so in the right spirit: ask the tree respectfully if you can cut some wood for your rune set and, once done, give thanks to the tree. In

the past it was customary to leave some form of payment for the tree in the form of a small, silver coin buried at the base. After all, you are taking parts of a living thing, and while the tree can easily spare a few, small pieces from its branches, the creation of your runes should begin in a spirit of dedication. You can use pieces of bark (although they tend to be too fragile for long-term use) or robust twigs to create runic "wands". If you find a large piece of beautiful wood you may carry it home and cut small blocks from it. Learning to work with wood can take a considerable time because it splits easily; work within the natural grain of the wood for best results.

Some people prefer to use stones. Smooth, rounded ones can be painted easily with the rune symbols, but will need to be sealed to prevent the paint from wearing away. Collecting stones can also be a spiritual occasion, although it is not quite so personal as choosing wood from a beloved tree. Choose your pebbles in the correct spirit, perhaps giving a word of thanks to the Earth.

If you are of an especially artistic nature you might wish to make a set of runes from clay. You can be immensely creative in this way and produce a personalized set. You are able to determine the exact size and shape of the runes to suit your own needs and can also paint them decoratively. Follow the guidelines in the next section. This could prove the most satisfactory method of all because the process of firing the runes, and in a sense burning in your own creative efforts, should empower them strongly.

It is also possible to create a set of runes from metal, although base metals would be a little too heavy in vibration to allow the forces of nature to flow easily. However, if you had the time, money and skill, there is no doubt that you could craft a fine set in silver, although this is probably best reserved for talismans and charms.

If none of the above appeals, you may even draw the rune symbols onto a set of blank cards and decorate them yourself. The only problem with using cards is that they cannot be thrown in the same way as more conventional rune sets.

marking on the symbols

Consider the proportions of the rune symbols: if you simply carve them to any, and different, sizes, they will lose much of their magical power and may even give expression to some of the darker sides of the universal force. In *Discover Runes*, Tony Willis explains how the essential geometry of the runes is governed ideally by a rectangle eight units high by three units wide. If you follow this rule it does not matter what size the symbols are as long as they are roughly in proportion to themselves.

Decide how to mark the symbols on. The easiest way is to use a felt-tip pen, but this does not give a very natural feel. You may, of course, use an oil-based paint and enjoy the certain magic that comes from using a brush to convey meaning to each rune as part of the ancient and much revered art of calligraphy. There is no doubt that carving the runes onto your chosen wood is the best idea as this takes considerable concentration of effort and thus adds to the strength of the runes. Keep a knife specially for the purpose of carving your runes so that it does not become imbued with the rather mundane vibrations of opening parcels or chopping vegetables. At all times work with a shape blade and always take great care.

Once you have made your carvings you could stain the wood. Use natural dyes if possible, and follow the traditional colouring: red for the most obviously male runes, and green for the female ones. Blue is a good choice for the cool or spiritual runes, and yellow for the mercurial ones. Perhaps the most powerful stain of all is your own blood. This act of sacrifice will certainly lend your runes another dimension of power but is not the right course for everyone.

If you are making your runes from stones, it is almost certainly easiest simply to paint the symbols directly onto the stones, perhaps following the colour codes above. Carving stones is possible, although not for the amateur. Make sure that you still follow the guidelines on proportion.

Whether you are using wood or stone, decide if you want to seal the runes with some sort of varnish. This is particularly important if you are using stone. Varnishing is very sensible and practical, but it does rather diminish the power inherent in the runes as you will feel as if their energy has been sealed in too. Remember that the power residing in your runes is determined by how close you, and they, are to the natural forces flowing through the universe.

consecrating your runes

The next step is to consecrate your runes – whether you have bought or made them. In our modern, rational society we have come to believe that anything "inanimate" – not moving about or talking to us – must by definition have no life energy. For example, we do not tend to see rocks as being alive and full of energy. Yet scientists now tell us that matter consists of energy – which can be neither created nor destroyed. This would barely come as a surprise to a shaman in ancient times. The fact is that everything is "alive" and has its own energy; some

things simply process energy at such a slow rate that we do not see see it, trapped as we are in our own energy time-scale.

Once we start to see the world around us in this way then consecrating runes begins to make sense because consecration is about transferring energy – from yourself into your runes. There is no hard and fast rule as to how to do this: you can devise a ritual that suits your own temperament and beliefs. You might wish to set up an altar and invoke the gods and their powers. Alternatively you may place your runes on your runic cloth (see page 82) and, kneeling in front of them, use all your intuitive and imaginative powers to embed the energies of the universe into your runes. Once you feel that the aim has been achieved, you can place the runes into their pouch (see page 82) for safe-keeping.

Creating a special set

If you have a particularly serious question you wish to ask the runes, you might like to create a set for that question alone. If so, you can collect wood from a tree at dawn, carve and consecrate the runes during the day, ask the question in the evening, and finally burn the runes at night before another day dawns. As this process takes an entire day it is probably best reserved for questions that are of critical importance to yourself or your client.

the runic pouch and cloth

In addition to your runes, you require two more pieces of equipment: a pouch and a cloth. You need a pouch in which to carry the runes and protect them from harmful vibrations and influences (in the same way as the traditional silk scarf protects Tarot cards). The pouch should be of simple construction and made from organic material such as leather, hessian (like the one supplied) or cotton. You may tie the pouch to your clothing so that the runes become imbued with your personal energy and are more responsive in readings. If you wish, you may put a great deal of time and effort into decorating your pouch, perhaps even embroidering a rune or two on the outside. As in all things, the more energy that is put into something and the more it carries your own personal touch, the better.

You will also need a cloth on which to throw, cast and shuffle your runes. The traditional colour of the runic cloth is white, symbolizing purity; it is also technically not a colour and as such does not have the same emotive effect as "real" colours such as red, blue and yellow. You can use any colour you wish as long as you bear in mind that it will always lend its own atmosphere to your readings. Choose a cloth of simple design: you are likely to find a highly decorated one distracting when you are giving readings. The size of the cloth is not especially important but, for ease of use, aim for one that is about 2 ft (60 cm) square. You might prefer your cloth, whether marked or not, to be circular, symbolizing more unity than the more pragmatic square.

The normal way to use the cloth is to swirl the runes on it and then select the required number (depend-

ing on the kind of reading you are making; see pages 104–127), placing them in their relevant positions, and then giving an interpretation. When giving readings, you could decide to lay the cloth facing a particular direction of the compass. This allows you to see in which direction the runes have fallen if you use a throwing method. For example, if the querent wishes to find out the location of a lost purse, and the rune of personal possessions and money falls in the eastern sector, this indicates the direction in which the querent should look. Once you become adept at this sort of reading you can also begin to understand questions of distance by how close together the runes fall. This takes considerable experience but, once mastered, can prove very helpful in a number of situations.

special cloths

You may like to keep more than one cloth for different types of reading. For example, if you like to give astrological rune readings (see page 122) it would be appropriate to have a cloth that has marked on it a circle divided into 12 "slices". If you prefer the older, square chart form to the circular one you could have that drawn on a cloth that you

keep specially for astrological rune casts.

Another form of cloth has three concentric circles drawn on it. This gives four separate areas to work with: the inner ring, the middle section, the outer ring, and the limitless space beyond. The outer ring in this drawing has been divided into four, but you could split it into any number of sections you like – for instance 12 astrological signs or 7 days of the week. Any rune that falls exactly into one of the marked sections would have a specific and clear meaning. The principle behind the concentric circles is to express the movement from spirit to matter. So at the centre is the entirely spiritual nature of the person or situation while on the outside is the physical manifestation, the effects on daily life.

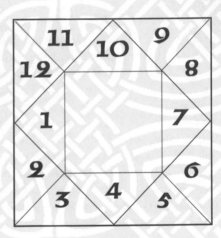

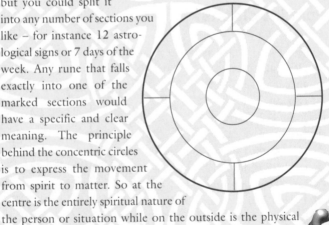

With marked cloths you simply place all the runes in your cupped hands, shake them around until they

are thoroughly mixed, and then throw them over the cloth, or let them drop from a distance that you find works best. This method leaves some of the runes off the cloth altogether; these represent the issues that are not involved at present. Those that remain on the cloth will be face up, face down, at an angle, upright and reversed. Using any throwing method requires experience and time, and a considerable number of trial runs to learn what works best for you. But with your own system your readings gain in complexity and you are able to exercise your intuitive powers to the full.

Runic talismans

You may wish to create runic talismans for a range of uses. For example, you could create a runic charm for good health that you wear on a necklace, carry a protective rune in your car, or have a wealth rune at your place of work. These talismans may be made either from single rune symbols or from several together making a runescript. If you choose to combine them you could lay them over each other to create a composite image known as a bindrune. This allows you to encapsulate your runic wishes in a very small space. The way you superimpose the shapes is up to you, giving you the freedom to be creative and artistic in your designs.

If starting a new business based on creative endeavour and located at home, you might select the following runes for your talisman: Ken to symbolize a new and positive beginning; Nied to show that hard work and effort will be needed to attain the long-term goal; Feoh to symbolize the desired increase in wealth; Ing to indicate the successful

85

completion of the enterprise and also prevent the business rewards being lost through carelessness or the actions of others. The rune-script would be as follows:

The bindrune might look like this:

Talismans like this make very attractive pieces of jewellery that look good to other people and carry an important message for you. One of the problems with creating charms such as these is that they are likely to draw attention from the cynical and merely inquisitive, so it is

always a good idea to find a method of incorporating your rune-scripts or bindrunes into your daily life in an inconspicuous way.

the numerology
of the runes

Over many centuries numerologists have ascribed a number to each
letter of our ordinary alphabet and by adding up the numbers in of
any given word or name they can reach an understanding of the qualities that held within that particular word. There is no reason why
this system cannot be applied to the runic alphabet. It certainly gives
another dimension to any runecast. In runic numerology, the system
by which the runes are ascribed numbers is slightly different from the
usual manner – in which the letters are numbered in alphabetical
order from 1 to 26, starting with A. In the system for numbering
runes, 1 belongs to the day of the Sun, (Sigel), 2 to the Moon, and
so on through the planets until Saturn is reached. Numbers 8 and 9
are generally believed to belong to the two wolves Skoll and Hati.
Nine is the highest number in this scheme.

The following list places the runes in alphabetical order with their
ascribed numbers:

The following list places the runes in numerical order:

ᛋ ᛗ ᛒ ᚠ ᚢ ᚲ ᚷ ᛏ
1 1 2 2 3 3 3 3

ᚠ ᚱ ᛉ ᛗ ᚦ ᛋ ᚠ ᚷ
4 4 4 4 5 5 6 6

◇ ᚹ ᛏ ᚾ ᚺ ᛗ ᛁ ᛉ
6 6 7 7 8 8 9 9

This numbering system can be useful for determining issues of time or distance involved in a question. For example, if you do a one-rune draw (see page x) when the question is, "I lost my ring, how far away is it?", and the rune Beorc is drawn out of the pouch then you know that it must be 2 feet, 2 yards, or 2 miles away. When dealing with time and distance you have to be flexible and use your intuition and common sense. For instance, if the querent is up for promotion and wants to know when it is likely to happen, and the result rune is Eolh it would be foolish to say 9 years.

There are of course several other ways in which the letters of the runic alphabet can be ascribed numbers. One is simply to number the runes sequentialy through the alphabet, making the first letter 1, the second letter 2, and so on until you reach 9 whereupon you start again so that the tenth letter would be 1 and so on through the entire alphabet. Wyrd is the "Joker" of the pack, and has no numerical value.

Using either of these numbering systems it is possible to create from a number of runes a single figure that gives an overall view of the runecast. For instance, a theoretical five-rune reading using the second numbering system might reveal:

$$7 + 1 + 9 + 2 + 6 = 25 \; (2 + 5) = 7$$

In this instance the underlying feel of the reading is symbolized by the number 7. By understanding the essential meanings attributed to each number between 1 and 9 you can gain more sophistication in your runecasts.

the symbolism of numbers

1 This is the primal force, the seed from which everything springs, the undifferentiated, single, unitary force. This number also denotes initiative and leadership and thus signifies the possibility of new beginnings. The number 1 also shows that the querent is extremely determined and tenacious in pursuit of their goals. This single-mindedness might

also show as narrow-minded conceit, so there is a warning here as well as a positive message. The querent will need to retain flexibility in order to achieve the best possible result.

2 This number symbolizes the primal energy of the universe dividing into polar opposites. At first glance the opposition implicit in duality augurs against co-operation, but both sides can be seen and heard, giving a great degree of balance and harmony. The number 2 is seen as a male number.

3 The triad has long been regarded as the most divine or perfect number, as expressed most clearly in the Christian Holy Trinity. *The Science of Numbers* points out that there are three dimensions of space – height, length and breadth; three stages of time – past, present and future; three stages of matter – solid, liquid and gaseous. Thus the number 3 represents a completeness, a totality. In everyday life this shows itself in terms of easy success. If the number 3 is the essence of a reading the outcome is almost certain to be highly provident. The only caveat is over-confidence. This number is seen as female.

4 This number is traditionally associated with the material world, with the descent of spirit into matter. It is represented by the square – a very unstable structure that requires triangulation to make it stable. The inference here is that the situation will require a great deal of effort to bring to a successful conclusion. There is tension inherent in the number 4 which can be used constructively if handled properly. Without due care and attention, however, the tension could prove too much and chaos ensue. This denotes a challenging time.

5 This number is traditionally associated with love, marriage and procreation. The union of the masculine 2 with the female 3 represents the creative impulse. In a rune reading, 5 may well denote a forthcoming marriage or birth, but on a number of levels, for example a new business venture or partnership. The number 5 is generally fortuitous but there is a danger of impulsive behaviour not based in reality. The querent has a good opportunity ahead but will need to keep a cool head and not get carried away.

6 The two intersecting triangles that represent this number make this an ancient symbol of the force of good. This number is perfectly balanced and implies that the querent is likely to see a very happy outcome to the present situation. Number 6 is also a very idealistic number so there is the possibility that the querent may undertake some form of altruistic work. Unfortunately, this idealism can also give the querent an unrealistic view of the situation that could prove quite disastrous if not tempered by pragmatism.

7 This has been regarded for many centuries as the most mystical of numbers. It is the highest primary number that can be divided only by the number one. It is the number of days in a week, the number of major musical notes in a scale, and was, until recent times, the number of planets visible in our solar system. The number 7 has many associations with spiritual affairs. When it shows in a reading it generally implies that there is both luck and wisdom surrounding the situation. On the negative side, it can infer that the querent has a tendency to remove themselves too much from life, preferring a slightly selfish solitude. The message here is to be a little more open and sharing.

8 This is the most solid of all the numbers; it is spirit concretized in matter. The cube has eight angles and may be regarded as the most structurally sound shape. The number 8 signifies that the situation will have to approached from a practical and efficient standpoint. This is not the time for creative whimsy or daydreaming; a tough and business-like attitude is needed. If this can be carried through, the chances of bringing matters to a successful conclusion are high. It is important, however, not to be so efficient and business-like as to become domineering, because there is a danger that you could ride roughshod over the feelings of others.

9 This number has some extraordinary properties that most people can remember from their school days. For example, if 9 is multiplied by itself or any other single number, the resultant two figures when added together always produce the number 9, for example 3 x 9 = 27 and 2 + 7 = 9, or 7 x 9 = 63 and 6 + 3 = 9. All the numbers between 1 and 9 added together total 45 and 4 + 5=9. Take any two sequential numbers, for example 54, reverse their order (45) and subtract the smaller from the larger; the result is always 9. There are many more examples of the peculiar qualities of the number 9, all of which show that it is in some way the most complete of all the numbers. This is as it should be, bearing in mind that it completes the cycle with the composite number 10 following after.

The appearance of the number 9 in a runecast indicates that there is a moral or philosophical tone to the current situation and that success lies in having the right attitude. A problem arises if querent takes a lackadaisical approach with their head stuck firmly in the clouds.

numerology in practice

When casting runes, particularly when using a throwing method, having an understanding of the numerology of the runes is particularly helpful. There is an easy method for making the most of it. Place your cloth on the ground and take all the runes in your cupped hands. After concentrating your mind on the question, stand up and shake the runes until they are thoroughly mixed. Then simply let the runes fall out of your hands onto the cloth. Not all the runes will land on the cloth. Discard those that have fallen to the side of the cloth and count the number of runes remaining. This gives you a final number that shows the essence of the situation being enquired about. For further information see the astrological reading on page 122.

preparing for a reading

Once you understand the philosophy behind the runes, have all the equipment you need and know how to interpret the runic symbols and their numerology, you are almost ready to start consulting the runes. Before you do, however, you need to prepare your mind and your body to be receptive, to have the correct attitude. One of the most important and effective ways to prepare yourself is by meditation.

meditation

Meditation is not some strange, arcane practice carried out only by oriental monks. It is a useful tool for bringing relaxation and letting you get in touch with your natural being. Meditation is essentially a state of calmness in which you let your body, breath and mind completely relax, without trying, without expecting anything. Being, not doing. Whatever activity is going on, recognize it and be still. Imaginations, fantasies, confusions, boredoms, doubts and questions drop away and you achieve a natural state of mind free from explanations and analysis. In time an inner awareness arises spontaneously.

Meditation begins by making everything tranquil, by allowing your body and mind to relax deeply and completely, by giving yourself warmth and nourishment. If you can be very calm and still and listen to the silence within your mind, this becomes your meditation. Even if you are not formally meditating, but just dealing with everyday situations, try to remain loose and relaxed. At first you may feel calm and peaceful, but a voice inside us, a speaker, a judge, rises to the surface and creates a disturbance and the inner silence disappears. You have to learn to let go of that judge. Within your meditation, do not think, do not act; thoughts come and feelings come but do not follow these bubbles. Let all your ideas and concepts disappear without becoming involved or trapped in their fluctuating dramas.

One of the most common meditation tools is visualization – creating a mental picture of something, for instance a particular rune, and then trying to concentrate on that image to the exclusion of all else. If you find yourself becoming distracted, observe and identify these deceptions, learn to see through the veil of your mind's posturing and pretences to achieve stillness.

The peace and stillness you find in meditation is

the universal flow of energy. This is the space where all barriers and separations disappear and only the force that connects all things is left. If we make an analogy with the potter's wheel, it is like throwing the clay off-centre only to find that it flies off and finishes up all over the walls. There is nothing wrong with either the clay or the wheel; the clay was simply thrown in the wrong spot. When the clay is thrown in the exact centre, making beautiful pots is not a problem. When you reach this state you will understand the power that is embodied in the runes. The runes will no longer be apparently dead stones but living conductors of the energies that flow through the universe.

ethical stance

It is also important before you begin to make sure that you have a correct ethical stance. If the runes are treated as a sort of party trick and handled without proper respect they will at best be of little or no value, at worst positively dangerous. It is not wise to treat the runes too lightly as they symbolize enormously powerful cosmic forces; understand exactly what is being unleashed. Since you as the rune reader are the channel for these forces there is every chance that you can let loose hitherto hidden, repressed or damaged parts of your own psyche with obviously disastrous results. As Michael Howard points out in his book *Mysteries of the Runes*, Odin himself warned against misuse of the runes:

> It is better not to pray at all
> than to sacrifice too much,
> a gift always looks for something
> in return, it is better not to send
> than to offer too much.

The message is quite plain. When you use the runes you effectively send out a great deal of energy that will in time flow back to you, greatly increased in power. It is therefore imperative that the original energy is of the highest level. This, in turn, requires correct thinking. Before playing with elemental forces it is vital to ensure that you are in a fit state to handle them properly. In this way the runes become much more than a divinatory tool: they are also a direct method to increase inner growth.

Consulting the Runes

When consulting the runes it always important to phrase the question properly; the act of meditating first helps to concentrate the mind. If your mind is muddled and unclear you can be certain that the runes will give you an answer that is largely incomprehensible. The more precise the question, the more precise will be the answer. Avoid asking multiple questions of one runecast. For instance, if the question concerned a new job it would be wise to ask, "is job X a good move?". If you asked, "should I become a designer, or a bricklayer, or stay in my present job in banking?", the answer would almost certainly leave you none the wiser. If you are giving readings to the general public you must impress on the client the need to keep their mind concentrated on the simple, core issue at hand.It might be advisable to set out the basis of every question in a few simple rules:

What is the subject of the question?
Who does it concern?
What period of time does the question cover?

These cover the essentials; with experience you will be able to create your own guidelines for outlining questions that help a client focus their mind on the fundamentals of their current situation. If doing readings for others you should not ask them beforehand what the question is: the runes themselves should make that perfectly clear. If you are aware of the question being asked before you cast the runes there is every chance that your own subconscious projections will prejudice the outcome. Your own mind must be totally concentrated on the task at hand. Let the runes do the work and always do your utmost to prevent any personal attitudes from obscuring the truth they reveal.

giving public readings

Once you are familiar with the runes and begin to do readings you will probably have to decide whether you wish to give readings to the public. This should never be undertaken just for fun but with serious intent. In "going public" you will almost certainly be surprised at the demands put upon you. Most people who seek a consultation with those in the divinatory trade are in a highly emotional, distraught and vulnerable state.

You will rapidly find that your duties extend far beyond the realms of simple runecaster. You will be obliged to assume the role of counsellor, psychologist, confessor and all-round shoulder to cry on. While the great majority of people are concerned with issues of love, money/career and health, and their questions will be fairly straightforward on the surface, on some occasions you will find that the querent is not actually asking the real question, that they themselves are in some way

97

unable to face the truth of the situation. If this is the case the runes will pick that up and display the reality behind the mask. If the runes are showing quite clearly that the question really concerns some other issue you will find yourself in the unenviable position of gently confronting the querent with the fact that they are not being entirely honest, largely with themselves. This is never easy to deal and requires great wisdom and sensitivity. If you feel that you would not be good at dealing with other people's problems on a regular basis, doing public readings is probably not for you.

Reading the Runes

There are a number of different ways of using the runes in a reading, but outlined here is one tried and tested way. In time find you will find the best method for you.

First of all, lay your rune cloth on the ground or the surface you are going to work on. Next, take out all 25 runes and lay them face up. This is a psychological process that allows you to see them all spread out before you to "fix" them in your mind. Then turn them all over and swirl them about in order to mix them up.

Some people have very strict ideas about which hand to use. Experience shows that in truth it does not appear to matter as long as the attitude is correct. Some people believe that the right hand is representative of the conscious mind and the left hand of the unconscious or psychic side of the mind. It is however generally accepted that swirling the runes in a clockwise direction generates the right sort of energy. This is an ancient belief that is manifested in many different divination systems. Even the Christian religion takes a dim view of walking

around a church "widdershins", which actually means contrary to the apparent motion of the Sun, the implications of which are obvious. Some experts on the runes suggest that a question requiring a positive outcome should use a clockwise swirl, while one seeking a negative outcome, such as "should I quit my job?", should utilize an anti-clockwise one. Once again, your own feelings and experience can help you determine which is best for you.

Once the runes have been thoroughly mixed select the number of runes you are going to use, depending on the type of reading you have chosen (see Sample readings, page xx-xx). This process is where your subconscious mind and your psychic "tuning" take over. Moving your hand over the assembled runes you will begin to feel that some of them almost "speak" to you, as if their inherent energy is jumping out at you, while others appear to be giving out little or no energy. Select those that emanate the strongest vibrations. Lay out your chosen runes in front of you. Turn over each of them, placing them to one side in the order of selection. Then replace the others in your pouch and lay out the selected runes in the fashion of the particular spread you have decided to use. You are now ready to start interpreting the runes.

the runes at a glance

The following two spreads act as a quick reminder of the essential meaning of each rune. Use this information to simplify initial readings or for making a shortlist of runes to carve as a talisman. For a more detailed analysis of the meaning of each rune, see pages 45–70.

Feoh symbolizes vitality and power, especially in the area of personal wealth and finances. The inherent strength of Feoh means it is good for any undertaking, for moving a situation onwards and upwards.

Ur is good for any enterprise that has a high risk factor. It symbolizes rapid change, the shouldering of new responsibilities, and the ability to sweep away obstructions.

Thorn is a powerful rune that can also be used in a protective manner. It is especially valuable when the querent is faced with circumstances beyond their control. It is the helping hand of fate that allows abrupt and potentially dangerous change to be overcome.

Ansur is the rune of communication and so augurs well for such matters as writing poetry, public speaking or passing exams. It is also good if there is either some learning that needs to be done or some test

that relies largely on personal magnetism and social skills.

Rad is a rune of travel and so is auspicious for all modes of transport and communication. It also rules travel in the broader sense of inner journeying. By virtue of ruling every type of travel, a degree of change is implicit in this rune.

Ken is a very positive rune that symbolizes the gentler acts of creation such as writing music or crafting talismans. It imbues all aspects of life with a protective and creative warmth.

Geofu is strongly associated with gifts – both giving and receiving. It is the act of giving that creates harmony in all things and this rune is especially auspicious when the subject is personal relationships.

Wynn is the ultimate happy rune, symbolizing the old adage "all's well that ends well". Like all good things, it is possible to have too much of it so a degree of restraint is also implied. Naturally it points to wonderful times in affairs of the heart.

Hagall is a rune that links directly to the primal forces of the universe; it can therefore be a little unpredictable. It can indicate frustration in some circumstances, but more generally points to the need to understand the precise limits of the particular situation and trust that luck will see you through. Such faith is usually rewarded.

Nied means precisely that – need. It implies that a situation has become blocked in some way and that it requires patience to resolve matters. Nied is excellent for the achievement of long-term aims. It does generally not augur well in matters of love and sex, and may indicate that bridges need to be built.

Is symbolizes "time-out", when matters have reached such a stage that to freeze frame for a while is the soundest course of action. It allows energy to rebuild which helps one to fight another day, just as winter allows the earth to rest before the growing phase of spring.

Jara is the rune of cyclical return when you can harvest the rewards of your actions. The word also implies legalities, and Jara is auspicious for all litigation. It can also symbolize birth, be it of a child, a relationship, or even a business.

Yr is one of the most mystical runes and gives direct access to the occult or spirit world. This power can be used in many ways but Yr is never evil. It is ultimately very protective, giving the power to remove anyone or anything that is creating obstacles.

Peorth is allied closely with all things hidden. Thus it is good for gambling and financial speculation, or investment of any kind. It is also good for finding anything lost, be it a physical possession or inner knowledge.

Eolh symbolizes protection in every form. Its shape resembles a lightning rod, drawing the life force down into the ground, or drawing the power of the gods into everyday life. This is a powerful rune, bestowing protection from enemies, increasing friendship and success in general.

Sigel is a rune that symbolizes the life force itself. It is the sun at the centre of the solar system around which everything revolves, and which brings life and warmth to the planet. Sigel is a very positive rune and bodes well for health in particular.

Tir, by its very symbol, is obviously martial, which implies that it is a "battle" rune. Tir is at its best whenever there is a difficult or antagonistic situation to be faced. It is naturally combative and will always seek to win any confrontation. The positive spirit it brings to life will help in recovering from serious illness or accident.

Beorc symbolizes a woman, womankind in general, or Mother Gaia herself. This is thus a very protective and nurturing rune with specifically domestic duties. Thus it is applicable to matters concerning fertility, children, spouse and family.

Eoh is another "change" rune. It is excellent whenever there is a need to alter one's circumstances. The change it signifies is not abrupt or unexpected and must be made carefully and within clear and prescribed limits. It defines the surrounding runes and makes the inherent flaws in the current position obvious.

Mann is a very humanistic rune that governs relationships. It is very efficacious for situations in which aid from others is required, or for any group enterprise, especially if it will benefit others. It also governs the rational mind and is good for times when learning, inventiveness or serious mental application is required.

Lagu is another female rune, allied closely with the creative process. It is valuable for any artistic endeavour, be it painting, music or writing. This rune gives the power to contact the side of human nature that is beyond the scope of the rational mind, so it governs the imagination and psychic powers.

Ing is a male rune but a partner to Lagu, and by association also a fertility rune. Ing is extremely positive and brings great power to any situation. It is an excellent rune for bringing matters to a satisfactory conclusion, but perhaps more importantly, it gives the power to retain the success that has been achieved.

Daeg represents daylight, implying that it is of great value when a situation needs to be seen from all angles. It is also very good for making a positive change, particularly in personal values and outlook. This rune shows that everything is out in the open and there are no hidden dangers in dark corners. In this way it represents security. Since the greatest aspect of human security is based on sound finances Daeg is generally accepted to be excellent for increasing financial standing.

Othel is a very earthy and pragmatic rune governing the family home, land, furniture and so on. It also governs all the activities in the domestic arena such as physical labor on or around the dwelling as well as gardening, and even care of the family money in terms of investments. As it represents family life and ancestry in general, it also governs care of the elderly, a traditional family responsibility.

Wyrd is a mysterious rune that tells the querent that they must accept what is to follow, the outcome is inevitable. This rune may signify a pleasant or a tough message depending on the surrounding runes.

casting and reading the runes

Whether you are casting runes for your own benefit, at the request of close friends or family, or as part of a public reading, you can choose how to cast and display the runes. Described here are seven different methods of reading runes – from picking out just one rune at random in a one-rune reading, to choosing 10 runes and displaying them in a particular design in the Celtic Cross, to throwing all 25 runes onto a cloth specially divided into 12 segments for a sophisticated astrological reading. You can use any method of reading the runes that you find suitable. You will almost certainly use different types of reading for different questions and will also probably develop your own personal variations too.

When giving readings, the outcome rune or runes may be very negative indeed, presenting a serious problem for the querent. If it seems as if the outcome is totally negative with no mitigating possibilities then creating a talismanic runescript or bindrune will go a long way to alleviating the negative energies in the runecast. By the same token, if the outcome looks positive then there is no harm in helping things along by creating a talisman or charm to reinforce these energies.

one-Rune method

This is the simplest method of consulting the runes; by implication the answer must be rather simplistic. Picking a single rune will not help you get to grips with the complexities of a situation but can be very useful for a quick, immediate view of the fundamental dynamic.

sample Reading

In this instance if you ask "what's going on in my personal relationship?" and you draw Peorth this clearly implies that things have been far from perfect recently but that it is more than likely that everything will come out in the open soon and be resolved happily. This might give you the impetus

PEORTH

to talk to your partner, knowing that the likelihood of success is high. Obviously if you drew a rune indicating frustration or delay then you would be wise to let matters lie for a while. For a single-rune reading it is not strictly necessary to spread out all the runes, turn them over, then swirl them around before choosing one. It is simpler to shake all the runes up in their pouch and then pick one at random.

three-rune method

This is another very simple method of consulting the runes and is best used for questions that require a relatively straightforward answer. It should certainly not be used for multiple questions. So a question such as "should I have the operation?" would be fine for the three-rune method, but if you asked "should I have the operation, and should I have it next week or next month?" the runes would not give an intelligible answer.

The simplest way to interpret the runes is as follows. Spread out your cloth and place all the runes face down on it. Swirl them around until they are thoroughly mixed, choose three and put them aside, and replace the others in your pouch. Place the three in a row and turn them face up. Then count the number of positive runes and negative ones. By virtue of the odd number there will always be a preponderance of one or the other. This will give you a direct yes or

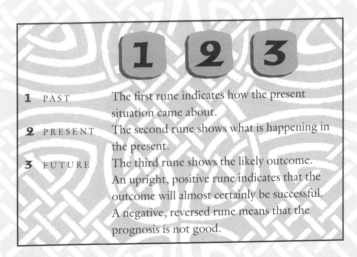

1 PAST	The first rune indicates how the present situation came about.	
2 PRESENT	The second rune shows what is happening in the present.	
3 FUTURE	The third rune shows the likely outcome. An upright, positive rune indicates that the outcome will almost certainly be successful. A negative, reversed rune means that the prognosis is not good.	

no answer. Two or three positive runes and the answer must be yes, only one positive rune and the answer must be no.

However, the three-rune method can also be used to give a reading about the past, present and future. Pick out your three runes one at a time and place them in a row, with the one you chose first on the left and the one you chose last on the right. You are now ready to begin the reading.

sample Reaðíng

In this sample reading you decide to ask the runes whether or not you should leave your job. The three runes you draw are Daeg, Hagall and a reversed

DAEG   HAGALL   ANSUR
                  REVERSED

Ansur. Daeg in the position of the past indicates that you have fairly recently benefitted from some extra finances. Hagall in the second position shows that things are not going well at present. A reversed Ansur in the final position symbolizes bad advice. You could interpret this to mean that you have recently come into some money and that you are looking to take a risk – presumably with the new money. Finally the reversed Ansur indicates that if you do take the risk it will be on the basis of bad advice. The answer is quite clearly no.

simple cross

This method expands the three-rune method to give a better idea of how the situation came into being, the stage it has reached and why, as well as the likelihood of it resolving itself. As before, spread out your cloth over the chosen area and place all the runes face down on it. Swirl them around until they are thoroughly mixed, put to one side the five you have chosen and replace the others in your pouch. Lay out the five runes in the order shown in the diagram.

sample reading

In this example you are enquiring about starting a new business and wish to know the likely outcome. Tir in the central position makes it clear that you are determined to make a go of things. It is, however, more than possible that you have been "baited" into making a potentially rash decision because the rune in the first position, Hagall, implies that forces outside your control are in some way forcing the issue. Perhaps you have been recently thwarted in some way and are now reacting to this. Lagu reversed in the third position shows that this decision will lead only to sorrow. The first three runes indicate that you are not approaching the planned venture with the right attitude. The Is rune in the fourth position indicates that the only way you can help matters is by keeping things just as they are. Jara in the

1 PAST	The first rune represents the past, what has led the querent to the current situation.
2 PRESENT	The second rune represents the present and should perhaps be turned over first.
3 RESULT	The third rune tells you what the result will be.
4 HELP	The fourth rune indicates what help is available to the querent. It can significantly affect the outcome.
5 OBSTACLES	The fifth rune symbolizes any obstacles that may be confronting the querent. This rune should be turned over at the same time as the fourth rune.

It is important to look at runes 3, 4 and 5 as a group. The outcome is not just waiting to be realized; if the querent understands the situation, sees clearly the obstacles ahead, and takes advantage of any aid available, then they can significantly alter the result.

fifth position implies that perhaps your current situation is far from bad and that you should invest a little more time and energy in it before making a change.

Overall, the thrust of the reading is clear: you feel like striking out and the advice is to wait until you are in a less reactive and combative frame of mind.

heimdales eight

This method of reading the runes is more complex than the previous ones. It gives a very detailed view of the querent's current situation and what has brought them to this point. There are four result runes, giving a thorough grasp of the dynamics of the outcome. Obviously this type of runecast should not be undertaken until you are fairly experienced as it needs knowledge and experience to practise effectively. Pick out 16 runes in the normal way, replacing the remainder in the pouch. Lay out the runes in their pairs as in the diagram. This is an excellent method to use when dealing with partnership issues because you can allocate the first rune of each pair to the querent and the second of the pair to the querent's lover, business partner, etc.

sample reading

In this sample reading we assume that you have been asked to make a reading for a middle-aged woman who is in inner turmoil. She has been married for 17 years, quite happily, and has two teenage children. Recently, however, she has fallen in love with a younger man and has become pregnant by him. He is a penniless, mature student. She has never before been unfaithful. She does not want to destroy her domestic harmony built over a long period but she does not want to give up her new love. Nor does she see how she can keep the child, bearing in mind all the circumstances, but she is morally and ethically opposed to terminating her pregnancy.

Ansur and Eolh comprising the first pair show that the querent, despite the current difficulties, has a good deal of inner strength and considerable diplomatic skills, backed by a warm and loving heart that will help her in resolving matters. The following pair, Yr and Rad, confirm the previous pair and clearly show that the querent is

1 & 2	STRENGTHS	The first two runes indicate what strengths the querent has available and how they might be used to solve the problem.
3 & 4	SYMPTOMS	Runes 3 and 4 show how the querent is coping with the situation physically, mentally and emotionally.
5 & 6	PAST	Runes 5 and 6 relate to the past and the underlying reasons that have brought the querent to this point.
7 & 8	OBSTACLES	The next two runes show what obstacles lie in the querent's path.
9 & 10	PEOPLE INVOLVED	Runes 9 and 10 indicate the people involved in creating the obstacles.
11 & 12	PRESENT	Runes 11 and 12 show what is happening in the present.
13 & 14	FUTURE	These runes represent the future.
15 & 16	OUTCOME	The final two runes focus on the likely outcome.

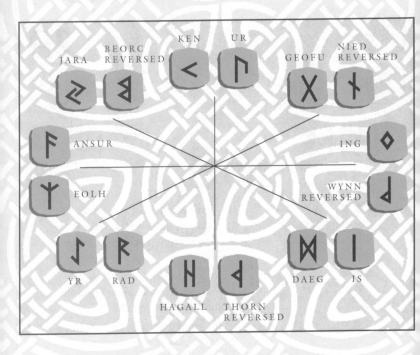

JARA BEORC KEN UR GEOFU NIED
      REVERSED   REVERSED

ANSUR   ING

EOLH   WYNN
                                  REVERSED

YR RAD HAGALL THORN DAEG IS
                 REVERSED

determined to find a way through using all her talents. She is very persuasive by nature and if she uses this skill fully it will certainly help. Runes five and six, Hagall and reversed Thorn, show what has caused the situation; they represent the new man in her life, with the reversed Thorn indicating how the querent has embarked on a dangerous course with little heed for the potential consequences. The next pairing of Daeg and Is suggest that the querent may well like to approach matters with a relatively sunny disposition but is likely to be met with a rather frigid response initially. A reversed Wynn and

Ing as the next pair indicate a mixture of unhappy termination and, at the same time, a feeling of relief.

It is now clear that a decision will be made soon – one that will almost certainly bring matters to a conclusion. Turning to runes 15 and 16 we see the likely outcome of domestic troubles and the possibility of legal separation as indicated by Beorc reversed and Jara. Runes 11 and 12 are Nied reversed and Geofu. The latter represents the husband in this context and the reversed Nied shows that the querent is likely to take a decision that will have very long-lasting consequences. The remaining pair are Ur and Ken; Ur represents change and new circumstances and Ken indicates a possible proposal.

It seems likely from this that the querent will choose to leave her husband. If she does, the consequences will be difficult and long-lasting, but she will most probably be very happy with her new man and their child, despite the financial problems they will face. The reading also indicates that while this decision will cause much pain and hurt for a considerable time, it is also likely that these difficulties can be overcome in time and some sort of harmony achieved.

celtic cross

This type of runecast is extremely old and widely used by Tarot card readers to this day. There is one slight difference between the runecast and the Tarot spread: in a Tarot spread the second card is laid across the first; with runes it is simpler to lay the second rune at right angles beneath the first. Although the runes are read in a specific order, it is acceptable to lay them out in a clockwise order. In other words the layout would be 1, 2, 6, 3, 5, 4, 7, 8, 9, 10. This is a matter of choice and experience.

sample reading

In this reading a question is posed by a woman who knows that her lover is seriously addicted to drugs, involved in crime to support his habit, and staring disaster in the face. The woman is unable to see how the situation can be resolved.

Ing in the first position indicates that, despite all the current evidence, there is hope for the future. The "crossing" rune, Wynn, amplifies this message. Wyrd in the position of the

2 IS UNDERNEATH 1

1 PRESENT	The first rune represents the current situation.
2 OBSTACLES	The second, "crossing", rune indicates the problems that present obstacles to resolution. Since this rune is horizontal it is wise to treat it as reversed since it is representative of negative trends.
3 PAST	The third rune indicates what has led to the present situation.
4 FUTURE	The fourth rune indicates what lies ahead.
5 AMBITIONS	The fifth rune represents the desires and ambitions of the querent.
6 INFLUENCES	The sixth rune indicates what has influenced the situation.
7 INTERNAL STRENGTHS	The seventh rune denotes what the querent brings to the situation.
8 HELP	The eighth rune indicates what others bring to it that can be of any help.
9 HOPES AND FEARS	The ninth rune traditionally indicates the querent's hopes and fears.
10 OUTCOME	The tenth rune symbolizes the likely outcome, although this has to be considered in tandem with the fourth rune, which indicates the future.

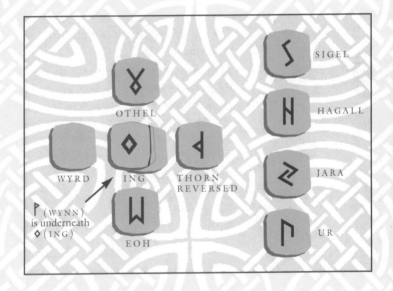

OTHEL

WYRD   ING   THORN
REVERSED

ᚹ (WYNN)
is underneath
◊ (ING)

EOH

SIGEL

HAGALL

JARA

UR

immediate past points to the likelihood of there being some price to be paid to put everything right. The reversed Thorn in the position of the immediate future could hardly be more apt as a symbol for the drug addict's needle. The implication is that the woman's lover is not ready to heed good advice. This is also indicated by the fifth rune, the reversed Othel. The sixth rune is Eoh reversed; in this context it implies that the person in question may have to go away before a resolution is reached. Whether this means voluntary admittance to a clinic or a forced incarceration will be shown in time. The reversed Ur as the seventh rune clearly shows that the lover has very little willpower at present and the rune in position 9, Hagall, further indicates that his general outlook is weak and gloomy. However, the runes in position 8 and 10 – Jara and Sigel – indicate that once the price has been paid there will be considerable aid available. The long-term future looks sunny with Sigel representing the outcome. Overall, the reading indicates the present weak state of the woman's lover and shows clearly that amends will have to be made and that good health and inner strength will return in time.

four quarters

This is a very interesting method of reading the runes when an outcome has more than one implication. For instance, if the querent is faced with the prospect of moving home the implications they have to consider could be having to move the children to another school and find another job. If the question is more complicated, perhaps concerning whether or not the querent should marry someone from another country, there will be more implications to consider. The enormity of the decision alone will be a concern as well as, if he or

11
CENTRAL POSITION
CURRENT SITUATION
This final rune, at the centre, describes why the querent has come for the reading.

1, 2 & 10
THE LEFT-HAND QUARTER
INNER STRENGTHS
The three runes on the left-hand side indicate what qualities the querent brings to the present situation

she decides to go ahead with the marriage, which country they should settled in and the need to become accustomed to a new way of life. This type of reading requires considerable experience as it involves groups of three runes as well as pairs of runes, so great degree intuition and synthesis will be called upon.

To begin the reading, prepare yourself and the runes in the usual fashion and having selected 11 runes, replace the remainder in the pouch and lay out the chosen ones as shown in the diagram.

in terms of inner strengths and weaknesses – physical, emotional or mental. The rune in the centre of this quarter, number 1, is the controlling rune of this triad and must be given greater consideration than the other two.

THE RIGHT-HAND QUARTER
5, 6 & 7 CURRENT DIFFICULTIES
The three runes on the right-hand side show the particular difficulties that the querent faces, and as with the first quarter, the central rune, number 6, carries the maximum influence.

THE TOP QUARTER
3 & 4 IMMEDIATE FUTURE
The two runes at the top, numbers 3 and 4, indicate the immediate future.

THE BOTTOM QUARTER
8 & 9 OUTCOME
The two runes at the base, numbers 8 and 9, symbolize the longer-term future or outcome.

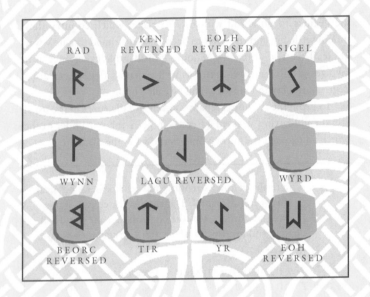

RAD · KEN REVERSED · EOLH REVERSED · SIGEL

WYNN · LAGU REVERSED · WYRD

BEORC REVERSED · TIR · YR · EOH REVERSED

sample Reading

In this case a couple come for a reading, concerned about the conflicts between their individual careers and their desire for children. Neither wants to give up their lucrative career to bring up the children; at the same time, neither is in favour of employing a nanny. Essentially, they are asking whether it will be possible to stay together with children and, if so, who will really be able to cope best with putting their career on hold.

The central rune is Lagu reversed, which shows that there is much unhappiness in the air. Unless the nettle is grasped immediately the situation could deteriorate further. Since this reading involves a couple it seems wise to allocate the first quarter to the woman and the second to the man. Runes 2, 1 and 10 on the left-hand side are Rad, Wynn and Beorc reversed, representing the psychological state of the woman. Rad and Wynn together show that she is genuinely seeking a way to be happy and is prepared to talk about things and make some compromises, while the reversed Beorc clearly points to domestic troubles. These three reflect the present situation accurately and confirm the need for understanding if matters are to be resolved positively.

The second quarter, runes 5, 6 and 7, are Sigel, Wyrd and Eoh reversed. Sigel shows the man as having considerable inner strength and Wyrd points to him reaching some stage in life where he has to face his fate head on. Eoh reversed indicates that change is imminent. The remaining runes should indicate what sort of change it is to be.

The top quarter, positions 3 and 4, show what is likely to happen in the near future. Ken and Eolh, both reversed, look very unfortunate as they indicate loss, separation and misunderstanding. If this couple are to create a happy future together they will certainly have to go through a period of painful adjustment that will test their patience and affection to the limit.

The final quarter, numbers 8 and 9, represent the longer-term future. Despite all the problems of the situation, the runes Yr and Tir, both in upright positions, clearly show that the result looks positive. In general, the couple should be able to resolve their problems, albeit with much pain, and reach a genuinely happy outcome. It also seems clear that it will be the man who will be staying at home to care for the child, a situation he has the strength to cope with much better than the woman, whose slightly more fragile ego would be unable to deal with what she would perceive as a loss of position in the world.

astrological

To effect this reading you need to have a cloth with a circle, or square, drawn on it that is divided into 12 sections according to the diagrams. This is a "throw" reading: place all the runes in your cupped hands, thoroughly shake them, then release them so they fall over the cloth. Retain only those that have fallen within the circle or square, and discard the rest. Then turn face up all that remain. Move any that have fallen across a "house" line into the house in which the

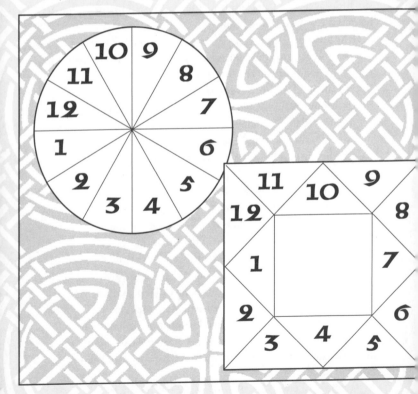

greater part of the rune has fallen. You will also have to make a subjective decision as to whether you feel a rune is reversed or not.

In order to interpret this type of reading you will need to understand the meanings of the various houses. Allying this knowledge with the symbolism of the different runes will put you in a position to give an accurate indication of the subtle dynamics that comprise the current situation.

FIRST HOUSE

This represents the physical appearance and the personality of the querent. It may also describe the precise circumstances that have brought the querent to consult the runes.

SECOND HOUSE

This indicates the talents at the querent's disposal. These may well be financial but may also relate to a more creative side that has practical applications.

THIRD HOUSE

The third house has much to do with travel, but only on a fairly local level, as well as all forms of communication. It also governs immediate family and especially siblings.

FOURTH HOUSE

This symbolizes the querent's family and home environment. It also denotes the parents, generally the father, but in some instances the mother. You will need to use your intuition in deciding whether the father or mother is represented if any runes fall into this house.

FIFTH HOUSE

This is the house of creativity, and in the most basic sense therefore, symbolizes children. It does, however, govern all aspects of creativity, so artistic expression comes under the aegis of this house. It is also associated with risky ventures in general and thus can often indicate gambling.

SIXTH HOUSE

This house governs health issues and also indicates a tendency to neurosis in the specific area of life designated by any rune falling in this part of the chart. It also symbolizes the day-to-day chores that comprise much of our lives. On a more positive note, the sixth house also governs attention to detail and the act of service.

SEVENTH HOUSE

This governs all overt relationships, particularly those involving lovers or partners of any kind, but also may indicate open enmity. In view of this, it can also relate to legal disputes.

EIGHTH HOUSE

Traditionally this house governs other people's money, so it often concerns wills, legacies and banking. The eighth house has much to do with things that are hidden and inaccessible, whether serious illness or investments that cannot be touched for legal reasons.

sample reading

In this case a man comes for a reading in a state of extreme distress as his 16-year-old daughter has run away from home and there has been no contact for almost three weeks. He is naturally concerned

NINTH HOUSE

Long-distance travel is the theme of this house. However, it may well not be literal physical travel but further education or personal, spiritual growth. This house is generally considered to bring good luck.

TENTH HOUSE

This house governs the ambitions and career of the querent. It symbolizes the way in which the querent realizes the traits handed down by their antecedents (fourth house). It tends to represent the mother but, as with the fourth house, you will have to make an informed judgement on this.

ELEVENTH HOUSE

This symbolizes the querent's social circle and their attitude to society in general. The eleventh house is a very altruistic and humanistic area of the chart. It may also show that a querent has political leanings.

TWELFTH HOUSE

This house has long been associated with loss, sacrifice and institutions such as prisons and hospitals. It is probably best known as "the house of self-undoing", giving it the association with incarceration.

firstly that his daughter is safe, secondly that she will return home, and thirdly about when this will happen. The runes are cast over the special circular astrological cloth. Nine fall within the circle; the other 16 are discarded.

The reversed Ansur in the first house implies that the father has perhaps not been listening to his daughter and that this might have

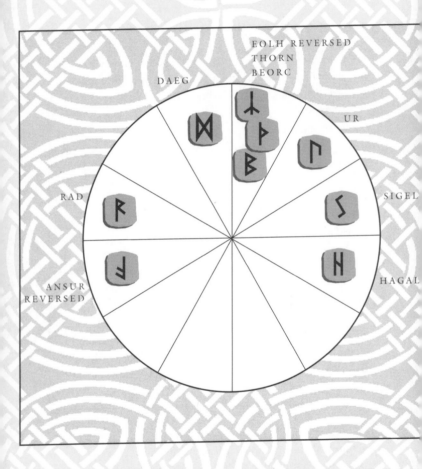

EOLH REVERSED
THORN
BEORC

DAEG

UR

RAD

SIGEL

ANSUR
REVERSED

HAGAL

126

been partly responsible for the current situation. Hagall in the sixth house shows that the querent has certainly had a great shock which is affecting his health. Sigel in the seventh house represents the daughter and shows her to be very much alive and well. Ur in the eighth house shows that she is also determined to prove herself regardless of the cost. This is a strike for independence and self-reliance. There are three runes in the ninth house, which represents travel and the learning process, amplifying the previous rune. These three runes – Eolh reversed, Thorn and Beorc – show that the daughter feels a little vulnerable but that she is well protected and will come to no harm. Daeg in the tenth house shows that the daughter is going through a process of change that will radically alter her own life and her relationship with the querent, her father. The final rune, Rad, in the twelfth house, indicates very obviously that the querent can expect to receive a message of some sort from his daughter very soon, probably in the form of a telephone call. Because Rad represents a wheel and the twelfth house represents the end of a cycle, it seems clear that the daughter will return home in time, but not before she has experienced what she feels is necessary, and also not before she feels her father has learned to listen to her properly.

Acknowledgements

The publishers would like to thank the following sources for their kind permission to reproduce the pictures in this book:

Ancient Art & Architecture Collection; et archive; Mary Evans Picture Library; Werner Forman Archive; Fortean Picture Library/Janet & Colin Bord; Mansell Collection.

Every effort has been made to acknowledge correctly and contact the source and/or copyright holder of each picture, and Carlton Books Limited apologizes for any unintentional errors or omissions which will be corrected in future editions of this book.